# Donald DeMarco

The War Against Civility
Copyright 2020 © Donald DeMarco, Ph.D.
Designed by James Kent Ridley
Published by Goodbooks Media
Printed in the U.S.A.
ISBN: 9798693143203

Signs of the Times
Copyright 2020 © Sr. Anne Marie Walsh, SOLT

GOODBOOKS MEDIA
3453 Aransas
Corpus Christi, Texas, 78411
www.goodbookmedia.com

# Dedication and Acknowledgement

This book is lovingly dedicated to our dozen grandchildren—Therese, Matthew, John, Michael, Paul Jr., Kierra, Lucas, Sophia, Marion, Hannah, Charlotte, and Lara—in the hope that they will always live their lives as model of civility.

The author wishes to thank the editors of *Adoremus, Celebrate Life, Catholic Exchange, Crisis, The National Catholic Register,* and *The Wanderer* for graciously permitting the publication of articles in this book that formerly appeared in their periodicals.

Alternate Titles to *The War Against Civility*: Discovering Order in a Disordered World, *The Death of Dialogue*; America at the Tilting Point; Can Catholicism Survive in Contemporary America?; *The Death of Dialogue*; America: Sweet Land of Incivility; *The Death of Civility*.

# Endorsement

Many of us deplore the huge crisis in our society today, but few of us have specific ideas about the underlying causes. In his remarkably cogent book, The War Against Civility, De Marco challenges us to renew our faith in the ideals of the United States. You will delight in his pungent style and be excited by his brilliant analysis. You will be amazed by the accompanying photos.

> Ronda Chervin, Ph.D., retired philosophy professor of Holy Apostles College and Seminary, EWTN presenter, and author of numerous Catholic books.

# Table of Contents

- 6) Forward
- 8) Preface

### ◦∽ Philosophy: ∾◦

- 17) Marching Back to 1984
- 21) Is Dialogue Possible?
- 27) The Philosopher in the Mass Age
- 31) Philosophy and Propaganda
- 35) Thought and Action.
- 39) Contempt for Authority
- 43) Following the Line of Providence

### ◦∽ Life: ∾◦

- 51) Does Life Have Any Meaning?
- 55) How to Flourish in a Fallen World
- 61) Baseball and Life's Pilgrimage
- 65) Open to Everything, Dedicated to Nothing
- 69) The Power of For
- 75) Meditation on a Peach Stone
- 79) With All Your Faults I Love You Still

### ◦∽ America: ∾◦

- 87) Monumental Principles From Dawn to Twilight
- 93) My Country Is My Identity
- 97) Geometry And Justice
- 101) Something Worse Than Racism
- 107) Vengeance Is Not Justice
- 111) The Submergence of Philosophy
- 117) Are We Still One Nation Under God?

### ◦∽ Catholicism: ∾◦

- 125) Deconstruction and the Incarnation
- 129) Can the Church Attract Converts in Today's Climate of Confusion?
- 133) Saint John Paul II Turns 100
- 137) The Media and the Mediatrix
- 143) Euthanasia and the Eucharist
- 149) Grace, Gravity, And The Search for Peace
- 153) Mary Is for Everyone

# Forward
# Signs of the Times

Cultural upheaval comes to every society as each generation strives to leave its mark, for better or worse. Pope St. John Paul II has called contemporary western culture a culture of death. What we may be watching with the current riots and civil unrest is something that can be likened to a kind of terminal restlessness. Anyone who has attended the dying knows what terminal restlessness is: It describes the end-of-life experience that manifests as pronounced agitation and restlessness. It can be caused by any number of things that are part of the dying process, from pain, to medication issues, to spiritual and emotional work going on inside the person.

Restlessness is already a general characteristic of our lives in time and it is present in the saved and the unsaved, the holy and the unholy. It is present in the individual but also in communities and nations. St. Augustine, in what may be his most quoted insight, reminds us that our hearts are restless until they rest in God. In the saints, restlessness manifests as a peaceful excitement or anticipation of the life to come. In the sinner, it manifests in agitation and anxiety that something isn't right, something important is missing.

The story of Nineveh from the OT is a lesson for us. On the verge of being destroyed for their sinfulness, the Prophet Jonah preached so effectively that everyone from the King on down repented with sack cloth and ashes.

They were spared but their conversion didn't last. They soon returned to their sinful ways and were visited once again by the prophet Nahum. This time they did not listen and they were destroyed. An alliance of conquered peoples attacked and destroyed the city which had been one of the greatest intellectual and cultural centers of its time.

Which way our society goes, depends on one thing and one thing only: repentance. Fr Michael Scanlan, Steubenville's former president and reformer, believed that repentance was the biggest need among Christians today. For joy and liberation, for salvation and preservation, for true progress, repentance is the only answer to the discontent and destruction generated by a sin-saturated society.

Nicolás Gómez Dávila notes that "Modern history is the dialogue between two men: one who believes in God, another who believes he is a god." The one who prevails in this now, very heated dialogue will determine whether we are witnessing the terminal restlessness of western civilization dying, or the labor pains of a new birth, a new springtime for the civilization of life and love.

> In the Heart of Our Blessed Mother,
> Sr. Anne Marie Walsh, SOLT

# Preface

Those who know virtue also know vice. This is because vice is a deprivation of virtue. The person at the top of the hill can see the valley. But those who are immersed in vice do not know virtue. As St. Paul states, "The spiritual man judges all things and whom no man judges" (*Spiritualis autem judicat omnia: et ipse a nemine judicatur*, I Corinthians II, 15). As a corollary to the Apostle's words, it is easier for those who are living a virtuous life to abide those who are not, whereas those who are not living a virtuous life cannot tolerate those who are. Christ came into the world to save sinners. Although His message is one of love, he was put to death. Pro-lifers want to convert pro-abortionists. However, the latter want to get rid of those who defend life. As New York governor Andrew Cuomo has said, there is no room in his state for people who have pro-life views.

Civilization is the crowning glory of civility-minded or virtuous people. As John Adams, America's second president wrote, "Liberty can no more exist without virtue and independence than the body can live and move without a soul". According to his presidential predecessor, "Of all the dispositions and habits which lead to political prosperity, religion and morality are indispensable supports." A war against civility occurs when a critical mass of people who have rejected the virtuous life violently turn against civilization.

Pornography, alcoholism, the use of illegal drugs, abortion, euthanasia, and widespread identity-theft are factors that tear at the fabric of civilization. The result is that society breaks down. The attempt to re-establish order, then arouses vengeance. Churches are vandalized, statues are desecrated, businesses are torched, and the economy falters. In addition, philosophy is abandoned, replaced by chaos and confusion. The horse is in the saddle riding man.

Be one of the small number who find the way to life, and enter by the narrow gate into Heaven. Take care not to follow the majority and the common herd, so many of whom are lost. Do not be deceived; there are only two roads: one that leads to life and is narrow; the other that leads to death and is wide. There is no middle way.

    St. Louis de Montfort

*Lord of the Flies* by William Golding

***Each new generation born is in effect an invasion of civilization by little barbarians, who must be civilized before it is too late.***
Thomas Sowell

*King of the Castle* by William Kurelek

*If you are not prepared to use force to defend civilization,
then be prepared to accept barbarism.*
Thomas Sowell

Lord of the Rings by J. R. R. Tolkien

# THE WAR AGAINST CIVILITY

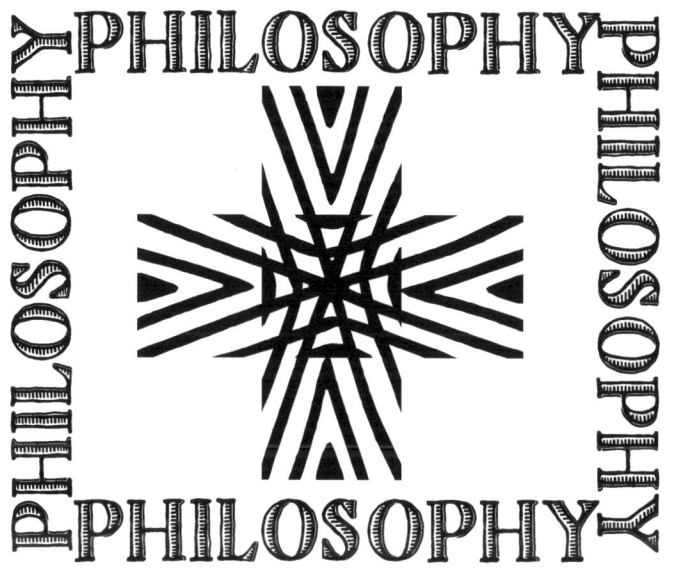

# The March Back to 1984

George Orwell's classic, *1984*, portrays a nightmarish dystopia in which people are not allowed to think: *"Thoughtcrime does not entail death: thoughtcrime is death."* An indication that its citizens do not think is that they simultaneously accept contradictory ideas, a mental aberration called "doublethink". This is the result of extreme indoctrination, something akin to what we now refer to as "political correctness". Hence, ***"War is Peace," "Freedom is Slavery,"*** and ***"Ignorance is Strength"***.

At the root of the totalitarian world that Orwell paints is the absence of philosophy. A person is free when he can open his mind to a reality that is not his own. A person is not free when the Party controls his mind. Although written 36 years ago, *1984* casts a powerful light on the present world in the United States in which people adopt doublethink and believe that love is hate, tradition is oppression, and right is wrong.

Today, philosophy is held in disrepute. It is either ignored, suppressed, unappreciated or scorned. Yet, it is indispensable for the continuation of civilization. Without a unified vision of reality, no agreement is possible, and, therefore, society plunges into the darkness of chaos and violence.

Philosophy is the love of wisdom. It begins with the mind aglow with wonder. How did the extraordinary richness and diversity of reality come to be? Why is there something rather than nothing? Wisdom is putting things in the right order, a virtue that has no end of practical significance. One should put his socks on before he puts his shoes on, one should learn medicine before he practices it, and one should earn money before he spends it. The opposite is said to be "preposterous," a most revealing word since it means putting "before" (*pre*) that which should come "after" (*posterius*).

***"The wise man sets things in order,"*** (*Sapientis est ordinare*) writes Saint Thomas Aquinas, citing Aristotle. This statement is fundamental to philosophy, for without order, chaos reigns. When St. Augustine states that ***"peace is the tranquility of order,"*** he is acknowledging the fundamental importance of philosophy.

Man's life should be set in the proper order. But man is a recalcitrant subject. G. K. Chesterton provides a sober and realistic image of him in the context of a theater production. It is as if God had written a play, ***"but which had necessarily been left to human actors and stage-managers who had since made a great mess of it"***. Man needs help in putting his life in order. And this is where the Good Book comes into play. It is an extended version of God's love for unruly man, telling him what he must do and what he must avoid.

People, however, can be resistant to being told what they should not do, even if the command comes from God. Love is the promotion of the good in a person. That necessarily entails telling a person that certain actions are wrong. As an inappropriate reaction, a person may believe that God, or anyone acting in his stead, is being hateful. By not approving transgressions, people think, God must be setting Himself against us. In this way, love is hate. It is not surprising, then, that more and more people are viewing the Bible as a form of hate literature and accusing God of hate crimes.

Tradition represents the abundance of good things I inherit just by being alive. I owe debts of gratitude to more people than I could ever acknowledge. Nearly everything I have, starting with my life, is something I did not create. I am essentially a pauper in comparison with the innumerable gifts that have been laid at my feet. Gratitude is my first response. My second response is dedication with the hope that I can contribute to posterity and in some sense be the recipient of its thanks. I hope that I can add to the tradition.

Unfortunately, instead of being grateful for every gift from the past, many people view the past negatively as a dubious contribution made by individuals who were seriously flawed. They feel that the vices of the past outweigh the virtues. They protest that tradition has stifled them. Therefore, they argue, tradition is oppressive.

Philosophy sheds a light on who we are as fallible human beings, how we should live, and how to give thanks for everything we have been given. It also show us how to distinguish between right and wrong. And yet, people can become riveted to their transgressions and stubbornly defend them as their right. Nowhere is this more apparent than in the area of abortion. Thus, pro-abortionists will insist that the truly violent people are pro-lifers who adamantly oppose a woman's right to choose.

Solomon is considered wise because he placed living above killing. Therefore, he ruled that the child should live and not be divided up between the two competing women. This form of wisdom is disputed today, since the continued life of the child is misinterpreted as the "death" of the woman. As a consequence, "right is wrong".

It is a most unhappy situation in America today that the children of wisdom, who see love as good, tradition as beneficial, and right as proper, are being ridiculed, and in some instances even arrested. The light of philosophy has not been extinguished; it has been neglected. In the confusion that rages about us, it remains an indispensable ally. The march back to *1984* and the adoptions of all its forms of doublethink is the march of misguided lemmings who are inching toward disaster.

# Is Dialogue Possible Any Longer?

The meaning of the word "dialogue" is to speak across (*dia*) the "*logos*". The "*logos*" refers to the source of reason that makes it possible for people to see the same thing. Reason unites because it is the common reality that binds people together. For Catholics, the "*logos*" is the "Word," and the Word was made flesh. The "Word," therefore, is the objective center of things, the source of reason that allows people who may initially differ, to come together in agreement. "Dialogue" is a word rich in implication and bright with hope.

Unfortunately, in this hour of mayhem, there is no center which can unite people. The Irish poet, William Butler Yeats described the situation quite accurately in his poem *The Second Coming:*

*Things fall apart; the centre cannot hold;*
*Mere anarchy is loosed upon the world.*
*The blood-dimmed tide is loosed, and everywhere*
*The ceremony of innocence is drowned.*
*The best lack all conviction, while the worst*
*Are full of passionate intensity.*

These words apply with dramatic and painful accuracy to what has been going on recently in Seattle, Portland, Chicago, Washington D.C. and other American cities.

The "*logos*" or the Word of God is our common ground.

Earth is also our common ground, and so is reason. Our feet stand on the ground of Mother Earth; our mind finds its common ground through the universal faculty of reason. We are, supposedly, rational animals. When St. Thomas Aquinas produced his monumental *Summa Contra Gentiles*, he stated his appreciation for the possibility of global unity.

> *Against the Jews, he wrote, we are able to argue by means of the Old Testament, while against the heretic we are able to argue by means of the New Testament. But the Mohammedans and the pagans accept neither the one nor the other. We must, therefore, have recourse to the natural reason, to which all men are forced to give their assent.*

Aquinas was wonderfully confident about the capacity of reason to serve as a basis for dialogue and the possibility for unity between all human beings. We find in today's world, however, that reason has been replaced by will, thus invalidating our rational faculty and converting society into discordant factions that are unable to communicate with each other. General Omar N. Bradley said it well when he made the comment that

> *Ours is a world of nuclear giants and ethical infants. We know more about war than we know about peace, more about killing than about living. We have grasped the mystery of the atom and rejected the Sermon on the Mount.*

There is, of course, much talk about dialogue and open-mindedness, but it is just talk. Reason operates magnificently when it comes to technology, but it seems entirely irrelevant when it comes to discussing pressing moral issues. The problem is serious and there seems to be no solution in sight. The frustration in not being able to communicate effectively often leads to anger, rage, fury, and ultimately violence. These unhappy consequences, nonetheless, are an indirect proof that human beings are made to be at peace with one another. There is a strong sense on the part of human beings that the path to violence is the wrong one. There must be a better way. Unfortunately, that better way—through reason—has been abandoned. The wrong note on the piano is wrong only because it is not the right note. We need to get back to playing the right note.

Shortly before President Trump arrived at Mt. Rushmore for an Independence Day speech, a native chief requested that the four presidents whose images grace the mountain be "removed". The notion spread like wildfire that the iconic figures represented "white supremacy". People began signing petitions for Barack Obama's face to be carved into the mountain. An issue that is born in irrationality can hardly be solved through rationality.

Washington, America's first president, united the country. Jefferson gave it the Declaration of Independence. Roosevelt opened the Panama Canal and was the first president to have an African American serve in the White House. Lincoln preserved the country, wrote the Emancipation Proclamation, and his Gettysburg Address stands as the most eloquent document ever written in defense of equality and democracy. Is there any reason to revile these individuals whose contributions to human rights is beyond compare? If we begin a conversation with a premise that is devoid of rationality, no resolution is possible.

Lincoln freed the slaves and honored people's religious

beliefs. Obama required the Little Sisters of the Poor to pay for contraceptive coverage, thus violating their strongly held religious beliefs. He was America's most pro-abortion president, consigning millions of unborn babies to premature death while claiming that killing the unborn is simply a form of health care.

Recently, a handful of black students at the University of Wisconsin-Madison demanded the removal of a statue of Abraham Lincoln from the campus. The university was founded in 1848, the same year that Wisconsin was awarded statehood. It has long been a champion of human rights, and offers special scholarships for black students. The protesters claimed that Lincoln's image was "offensive". If the most towering figure in American history is now seen as offensive, then all images of Americans should go with him. Is it reasonable to demand the eradication of American history? Is this a discussable matter?

How do opposite sides come to terms in this Wild West moment of history? I commend *The Wanderer* for doing what it should be doing, which is standing firm for reason, while hoping that reasonable discussions that may bring about agreeable solutions and even form the basis of friendships. There is no other reasonable choice. Through reason we become free; from reason, we become enslaved.

Sack of Rome, 410 AD

Sack of Russia, 1917 AD

Sack of Portland, 2020 AD

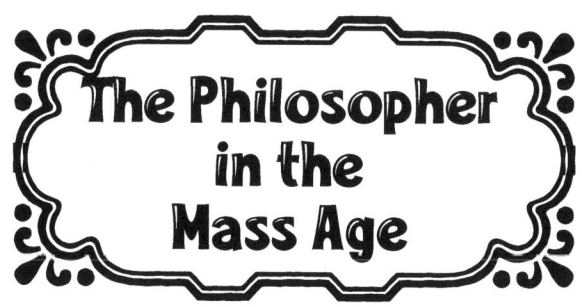

# The Philosopher in the Mass Age

Gabriel Marcel's book, *Man against Mass Society* (1952), is a reaffirmation of the fact that good philosophy is never irrelevant to the times in which we live. Marcel's thesis is twofold. On the one hand, it examines the phenomenon of *"mass society"*. On the other hand, he explores the duty of the philosopher. These two concerns represent the very opposite poles of the human spectrum.

His analysis of the masses is unsparing, yet insightful and vitally needed.

> *The masses are of their very essence—I repeat, of their very essence—the stuff of which fanaticism is made: propaganda has on them the convulsive effect of an electric shock. It arouses them not to life, but to that appearance of life which particularly manifests itself in riots and revolution.*

Historically, and psychologically, he is on good ground. Viktor Frankl has written about *"psychic epidemics"* that are possible causes of war.

The current riots, especially in various cities throughout the United States that are, ostensibly, a reaction to police brutality, represent the phenomenon of a mob fueled by propaganda. For Marcel, who is the founder of a French school of

Catholic existentialism, such occurrences portray the masses *"at a level far below that at which intelligence and love are possible."* Marcel holds little hope in communicating with the masses. And yet, he is an apostle of hope. *"I am inclined to believe that hope is for the soul,"* he writes in his book, *Homo Viator, "what breathing is for the living organism"*. His hope rests on the goodness of God and the inherent potential for goodness in man.

What is the duty of the philosopher, asks Marcel. "Without any possible doubt," he states, "it is that I ought not to sin against the light." His thought in this regard is linked to the Gospel according to John: "That was the true Light, which lighteth every man that cometh into the world". The richness of this passage, for Marcel, is of *"unsurpassable adequacy that is in fact the most universal characteristic of human existence"*. A person, therefore, is not fully a person, unless he is enlightened by that light.

This "light," which comes from God, is realized at its upper limit as Love and Truth. A truth that lies below this limit is a pseudo-truth. Love without truth is "a mere delirium". We presently witness injustice parading as "justice," violence pretending to be "peaceful". If the philosopher's first duty, in the negative sense, is not to sin against the light, that same duty, in a positive sense, is to radiate this light for the benefit of each other. We have this capacity. We are derelict if we do not cultivate it.

In the Marcellian sense of the word "philosophy," we can all be philosophers. This notion offers great hope. Marcel is often referred to as a "Neo-Socratic". Socrates was not an academic. Unfortunately, philosophers, according to the popular perception, are to be found only in the university classroom. And even then, most of those who claim a philosophical education teach not philosophy but its history, or even worse, repudiate philosophy, replacing it with relativism, cynicism, skepticism, or nihilism.

Seven years after the publication of Marcel's *Man against Mass Society*, George Grant wrote *Philosophy in the Mass Age*. At one time Grant was regarded as Canada's most outstanding philosopher. His status suffered considerably, however, when he defended the unborn. He was unwilling to conform to the Zeitgeist, and also unwilling to ignore the lives of the innocent. He wrote:

> ***The dying out of careful philosophical study in Canada is one factor helping to produce our dead-level, conformist society. When people have not thought about ideas quite different from their own, they tend simply to live within the principles of their civilization, not even conscious that they are living within those limits.***

The masses conform to a single idea and are highly susceptible to propaganda. The American media has assumed the role of fueling the masses with dubious ideas and omitting important facts. For example, David Dorn, a black retired  police captain, spent 38 years with the St. Louis Metropolitan Police Department. He was helping out the owners of Lee's Pawn and Jewelry store when he was shot to death by a looter. The assailant, 24, and also black, has been taken into custody and charged with first degree murder, first degree robbery, first degree burglary and the illegal possession of a firearm. The media coverage was either scant or non-existent. No media coverage was allowed inside the church during Dorn's funeral services. His demise, virtually unreported by the mass media did not fit into its specific propaganda interests. His passing did not matter in the ideological sense.

Marcel is a convert from atheism to Catholicism, which is to say, from nihilism to Love and Truth. He continues to radiate his values through his many books. Marcel has a special gift for personal reflection. And he also has the ability to awaken his readers to personal reflections of their own. Etienne Gilson has said that

> *Marcel is always assured of a circle of readers. In his work, man is directly in conversation with man: it will always have readers, because he will never cease to make new friends.*

In the final analysis, we all feel drawn to opposite poles: one toward conformity with the masses and the loss of personal uniqueness, the other toward personal authenticity and to God. Marcel engages his readers with the hope that they will follow the latter. He is horrified, as we should all be, of the former.

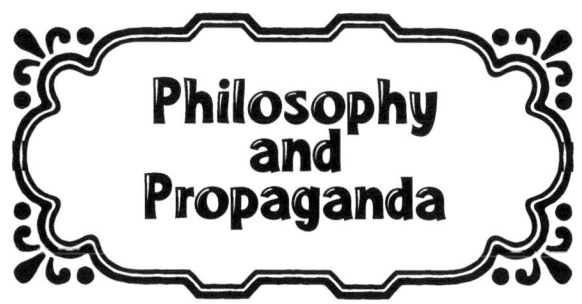
# Philosophy and Propaganda

On May 25, 2020, the Calgary, Alberta city council passed a "conversion therapy" bill by a vote of 14-1. According to the bill, any counselor who offers to reduce a person's same-sex attraction or reaffirms a person's birth sex is subject to a fine of up to $10,000. The by-law also applies to anyone making such an offer in a private conversation or during a public sermon. One of the councillors proposed an amendment that would allow conversion therapy to a person who freely choses it. The amendment, however, was defeated.

It seems odd that a homosexual who wants to rid himself of unwanted same-sex attractions would be denied in the interested of protecting his freedom. Treatment is routinely offered for people suffering from addiction to drugs, alcohol, and even food. Why not offer similar treatments for people (homo-or heterosexual) who are addicted to sex? The bill may be unconstitutional and tested in the courts.

Apart from civil law implications, the Calgary bill represents a dismissal of Genesis. A person is now subject to heavy financial penalties for citing that "God made them male and female" and marriage is the union of a man and a woman. How did the Calgary councillors surpass the Bible in moral wisdom? People can shift from one sex to another, but not from one sexual orientation to another. There is more than a hint of discrimination here. This new wisdom might not enjoy a long life.

In addition to the Draconian quality of the bill, what stands out on my mind is its overwhelming approval. An 80% agreement on a bill of such dubious implications certainly arouses suspicion. Only a few years no Calgary councillor would have approved such a bill. How do times change so dramatically and so quickly? We see similar radical shifts in thought concerning abortion, euthanasia, same-sex marriage, as well as homosexual activities. Philosophy should not be as unstable as changes in barometric pressure or the fluctuations of the stock market. It should be an anchor that gives society a certain stability.

Philosophy is concerned with pursuing the truth. Stating such a quest these days appears to be presumptuous. Yet nothing serves us better than truth. And if truth is difficult to attain, it should not be abandoned for that reason. In sports, one either wins or loses. But no one can win if he does not play the game. In the game of life, Truth is our North Star.

Philosophy requires a positive activity of the mind. Being a passive subject to the Zeitgeist requires no effort. Hence, we come to the difference between philosophy and propaganda. Economist Thomas Sowell makes an important point when he states that

> *If people in the media cannot decide whether they are in the business of reporting news or manufac-*

*turing propaganda, it is all the more important that the public understand that difference, and choose their news sources accordingly.*

His caveat should be taken seriously.

Christ has told us that the truth shall make us free (John 8: 32). But the truth, like philosophy, requires continuous effort. Anybody can be trendy. Being mesmerized by the media is sufficient. Incomplete ideas that float on the wind are absorbed unconsciously. It is akin to being possessed by alien forces. The dreaded Covid-19 virus is invisible yet harmful. It passes from one person to another in ways that are mysterious. It renders us passive. The same can be said for bad philosophy that is transmitted through incomplete ideas (like choice without consequence, sex without marriage, or education without truth). The Covid-19 virus and bad ideas are both contagious. And it is debatable as to which generates more harm. Bad ideas, of course, have had a much longer inning. The former is air-borne, the latter is transported on the wings of propaganda. In the world of academe, we have reason to wonder if studies centering on diversity, feminism, and gender equality are truly educational or merely forms of propaganda delivered under the pretext of education. Playwright and Nobel Laureate Harold Pinter has made the comment that *"It is so easy for propaganda to work, and dissent to be mocked."* Thus, Catholics are mocked for adhering to the truth of the unborn, and holding to the authority of the Bible.

G. K. Chesterton has reminded us that *"A dead thing can go with the stream, but only a living thing can go against it."* Trendiness streams into our minds without our realizing it. We may think we are being liberal because we are celebrating something new, but we are being iconoclastic because we fail to see the value in something old. Propaganda replaces thinking, philosophy energizes it.

The 2011 film, *Contagion*, is about a deadly virus that sends the entire world into a panic. It has been hailed as

"The film that anticipated our pandemic". The horror of both pandemics lies in the fact that they render us helpless. Yet there is another contagion that is going on, one in which our minds are infected with propaganda. Concerning this one, there is something we can do to oppose it, namely, to develop a love for truth and pursue it vigorously. Truth, in the final analysis, will be our most effective weapon in fighting the Covid-19 pandemic. We cannot allow ourselves to remain passive to both the Covid-19 virus and the reality of truth.

# Thought and Action

A physicist friend of mine told me that one of his students wanted to become a physicist but hated mathematics. My colleague laughed at contradiction. This odd separation of ends from their indispensable means is, however, not all that unusual. All my students, for example, want to be happy, but a rather small percentage of them a willing to accept the means necessary to attain that desirable end. Here is one of the great paradoxes of life: the concrete stands on the shoulders of the abstract. Therefore, it is so easy for students to separate them from each other, the former being evident and tangible, while the latter remains hidden and intangible. Nonetheless, as reason tells us, an unseen God created the visible world. Can we deny the Creator his existence?

This separation of ends from their means can be associated with a similar separation of action from thought. It is all too common for people, seeing little value in philosophy, to deplore certain actions while remaining indifferent to the very thoughts upon which they rely. This is a most serious problem since philosophy gives us the enlightenment we need in order to prevent the emergence of deplorable actions. Philosophy, though intangible, is extremely practical when it is properly applied.

I am utterly fascinated, therefore, by how people can protest against certain actions without protesting against the very ideas that contribute directly to those actions. The example of Dietrich von Hildebrand and his wife, Alice, well  illustrates the point. Dietrich had both the intelligence and the courage to speak out against Hitler and Nazism. His strong and well circulated objections earned him the distinction of being the number one enemy of the third Reich. A warrant was issued for his assassination. Through the assistance of many friends, he fled to Austria, then to France, to Portugal, to Brazil, and finally to the United States where he began a teaching career in the philosophy department at Fordham University. According to his wife,

> *My husband's ardent love for truth is what allowed him to perceive the poison of the Nazi philosophy so quickly. When truth was violated, it registered clearly to someone who had such an appreciation for it.*

Von Hildebrand's philosophy is essentially anti-Nazi. Moreover, the root of his philosophy lies in the fundamental value of truth. In a chapter entitled "The Dethronement of Truth," in his book, *The Tower of Babel* (1953), he refers to a the Bavarian minister of education, a certain Hans Schemm, who made the following astonishing statement before an assembly of university professors:

> *From this day on, you will no longer have to examine whether something is true or not, but exclusively whether or not it corresponds to the Nazi ideology.*

In this way, no one has any basis from which he can denounce Nazism. An ideology without a justifying philosophy is something that any intelligent person should reject. It is truth that determines whether a position is right or wrong, and certainly not the biased sentiments of the Nordic race. Dethrone truth and war becomes inevitable. Von Hildebrand records his courageous stand in his book, *My Battle Against Hitler: Faith, Truth and Defiance in the Shadow of the Third Reich.*

Von Hildebrand's wife, Alice, brought her husband's anti-Nazi philosophy to Hunter College, where she taught philosophy for 37 years. In her autobiography, *Memoirs of a Happy Failure* (2014), she recounts how she was persecuted for disagreeing with the dominant school of relativism. Harvard law professor, Mary Ann Glendon, attests that *"Her love of truth shines forth on every page of this fascinating personal Memoir"*. But her commitment to truth was her greatest obstacle. In fact, she was told by her school administrators not to teach objective truth. It took 15 years for Hunter College just to give Alice her own desk. *"Someone – God – wanted me there,"* she writes. *"After 13 years I was granted tenure,"* she recalls, by a 9 to 8 vote, passing an unprecedented Gestapo-like interview of two hours by 15 heads of departments and two deans. She and others as well regarded her being awarded tenure as a "miracle". Not everyone shared this view, however. Astonishingly, even rabbis, several of them in fact, protested against her being granted tenure. *"In secular universities"* as Alice observes, *"the word 'objective truth' triggers panic."*

How can it be that Nazism is universally denounced, while the very ideas that spawned it not only remain free from criticism but those who bring it to light are censured? Relativism produces an atmosphere in which ideologies like Nazism thrive. The answer may be complex, but surely one of the key factors is a separation of thought from action, means from ends, cause from effect, or philosophy from life. Alice von Hildebrand, like her distinguished husband, was a philosopher. For this she paid the price. But she also reaped the harvest, particularly in the joy of knowing that her teaching inspired and guided many of her students into the Catholic Church. In 2013, Pope Francis formally recognized her as a Dame Grand Cross of the Equestrian Order of St. Gregory in recognition of her lifetime work on behalf of the Church.

Alice von Hildebrand and her husband Dietrich devoted their lives to a philosophy that rested on three points: reverence, value, and God. When we have reverence for the natural values of life, including human life itself, we are moving in the direction of God who created all things that are good and thereby inscribed with value. In her biography of her late husband, *The Soul of a Lion* (2000), which resonates with their shared philosophy, including their mutual opposition to abortion, she records his final words: *"A country that legalizes murder is doomed."* If abortion is the dethronement of truth, then we are surely doomed.

# Contempt for Authority

Renowned neurosurgeon, Dr. Benjamin Solomon Carson, Sr., offers some badly needed wisdom when he speaks about the vandalism, looting and other forms of anti-social behavior that seem to be escalating in the United States. The remedy to the problem, he states, lies within the family. Unfortunately, as he avers, *"it is almost politically incorrect to talk about family values"* (Fox News July 15, 2020). He cites the fact that so many young people grow up in today's society without a father figure, someone to teach them to think of the welfare of others.

Carson should be taken seriously. The concept of the family, given the influence of the LGBTQ movement and other organizations that demean the nuclear family, has become nebulous and undefinable. On the BLM website we read that its members

> *"foster a queer affirming network. When we gather, we do so with the intention of freeing ourselves from the tight grip of heteronormative thinking, or rather, the belief that all in the world are heterosexual (unless s/he or they disclose otherwise)."*

Political correctness is both a major cause of the current problem as well as a preventative for its solution. It is arbitrary, inconsistent, ideological, and heartless. Scholar Jacques Barzun has remarked that

> *... the working of 'political correctness' in universities and the speech police that punishes persons and corporations for words on certain topics quaintly called 'sensitive' are manifestations of the permanent spirit of the inquisition."*
> **(From Dawn to Decadence, p. 109)**

There is no forgiveness for those who violate the canons of political correctness.

I would like to elaborate on Dr. Carson's point. Study after study indicates the importance of the father in teaching his child respect for authority. St. Thomas Aquinas makes a very important point when he states that the respect that one has for the rule follows naturally from respect that one has for the one who gave it *(ex reverentia praecipientis procedere debet reverentia praecepti*, S.T. II-II a, 2).

A father is an authority, but a loving authority who has inspired trust in his children. We are speaking here, of course, of the way a father should be. When he teaches his son about the fundamentals of baseball, he will say, "Hold the bat firmly with your right hand about your left hand, maintain the proper distance between your feet, and always keep your eye on the ball." His son accepts his authority with trust because he knows it was given with love. The father-son relationship teaches respect for legitimate authority. The child will be prepared to distinguish authority which frees from authoritarianism which enslaves. He will develop a close bond with his father because he knows that his father's words are more trustworthy than those of public opinion.

Authority that is detached from personality is cold and abstract. It has diminished power to inspire. In the context of a loving family, however, it seems normal and natural. Children are not born virtuous. As a pundit once said, "A child will learn his moral values from his mother's knee or at some other joint".

Authority is freeing. Consider the authority of the dictionary, for example, which allows people to communicate intelligibly to one another. If I use the word "hello" instead of "help," I cannot summon help when I am in distress. If, in a bold expression of freedom, I always use "no" instead of "yes," people will soon come to distrust me and will exclude me from their social circle. In obeying the authority of the dictionary, I am free to engage in meaningful conversations.

The fact that legitimate, loving authority is freeing is something that children must learn. And the most natural and logical place to learn this lesson is in the family, which John Paul II often referred to as the first school of learning.

Aquinas maintained that it is a lesser sin to reject the law than it is to reject the person representing the law. Because respect for the law flows from respect for the person representing the law, rejecting person disrespects both the person as well as the law.

Parenthood carries with it awesome responsibilities. Defects in the character of mom or dad, hinder their ability to convince their children about the differences between right and wrong and to live by what is right. Children understand intuitively that the reliability of an authority is deeply connected with his moral character. Studies have also shown that juvenile delinquency rises in direct proportion to the decline of moral values among parents.

Aristotle was making the same point when he said that a speaker should first render his audience benevolent. Kindness begets kindness. We must establish a warm human relationship with others before we can expect that anyone will take us seriously. A classroom teacher must establish trust first before he has a chance to get his point across. His message, ultimately, may not be accepted. But that is not the point. He must be trusted before he can expect a faith hearing, and I suppose, that is all a teacher wants from his students.

On a theological level, we find an important message in the statement, *"The Word became flesh and dwelt amongst us"*. Christ's authority is never abstracted from His Personality. Therefore, he becomes a model of trustworthiness. His words are inscribed in his being as well as in his love. Respecting the legitimate authority of the father makes for an easy transition to accepting the authority of God. The family, consisting of mother, father, and children, remains un-improvable and irreplaceable. Contempt for all authority reduces a person to being a cosmic orphan.

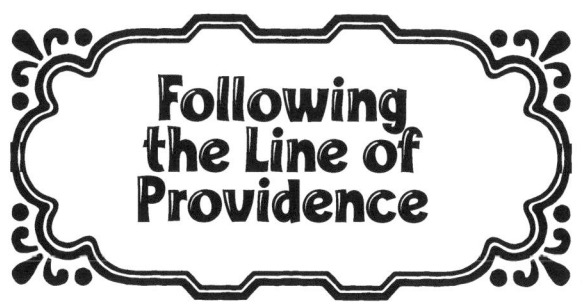

# Following the Line of Providence

The cynic will deny the existence of Providence. That is because he wants to be the sole master of both his dowry and his destiny. What he does not realize is that God has, so to speak, beaten him to the punch. It was God, not he, who granted him existence, placed inclinations in his being, and provided him with the means to fulfill those inclinations. We do not invent our destiny, no more than we choose our parents and our place of birth. We pursue it. Without God, we can do nothing.

During Black History Month, it is most fitting to recall how Wilber Wilberforce (1759-1833) saw his role as fulfilling the providential duties that God had given him. Far from being self-centered, Wilberforce believed that the great choice he had to make in life was between self-interest and something much larger in working for God.  As he stated in his diary, "My walk is a public one. My business is in the world, and I must mix in the assemblies of men or quit the post which Providence seems to have assigned me."

Wilberforce was an Evangelical Christian and one

of the leading Abolitionists in England who fought unremittingly against slavery. "So enormous, so dreadful, so irremediable did the trade's wickedness appear," he wrote, "that my own mind was completely made up for abolition. Let the consequences be what they would: I from this time determined that I would never rest until I had effected its abolition." The work of the Abolitionists proved successful and led to the *Slavery Abolition Act of 1833* which abolished slavery in most of the British Empire. Wilberforce died just three days after hearing that the passage of the Act through Parliament was assured.

The attitudes of Wilberforce and Abraham Lincoln toward slavery were strikingly similar. The former held that everyone should live "by the golden rule of doing to others as in similar circumstances we would have them do to us." The latter affirmed that "As I would not be a slave, so I would not be a master." In this regards, they both upheld democratic values.

God has left the final carrying out of his Providential Plan to us. Some cooperate; others do not. We are given our life, our appetites, and the means of directing them to their proper ends. When we accede to these gifts, Providence becomes evident to us. As Blaise Pascal once wrote,

> **He that takes truth for his guide, and duty for his end, may safely trust to God's providence to lead him aright.**

In America, Jackie Robinson is honored as the first black baseball player to cross the color barrier. This particular crossing, however, would not have taken place without the vision, determination and courage of Brooklyn Dodger executive, Branch Rickey (1881-1965), who, like Wilberforce before him, was a man of deep Christian faith. Rickey, who played professional football as well as baseball, detested racism and was determined to do what he could to overcome it. *"I may not be able to do something about racism in every field,"* he once stated, *"but I sure can do something about it in baseball."*

In 1847 Jackie Roosevelt Robinson, thanks to the assistance of Branch Rickey, made his baseball debut for the

Brooklyn Dodgers. He was named baseball's first "Rookie of the Year" and led his team to the World Series. Though he was jeered by opposing players, managers, and fans, he was extremely popular with the American public. For Mr. Rickey, his role in opening the door for blacks to play in the Major Leagues was the crowning achievement of his illustrious career and a key factor in his election to baseball's Hall of Fame.

Branch Rickey was a thinker as well as a doer. He knew that if Providence was to be fulfilled, people had to apply themselves to the God-given laws of reality. *"Things worthwhile generally don't just happen by chance,"* he once stated.

*Good luck is what is left over after intelligence and effort have combined at their best. The law of cause and effect and causality both work the same with inexorable exactitudes. Luck is the residue of design.*

No doubt, Rickey would have applauded these words of Martin Luther King, Jr.:

*I refuse to accept the view that mankind is so tragically bound to the starless midnight of racism and war that the bright daybreak of peace and brotherhood can never become a reality... I believe that unarmed truth and unconditional love will have the final word.*

From a philosophical perspective, "fortune" may be a better word than "luck". We are fortunate to have a providential God. One may cite one illustrious example from history. Giovanni Fidanza (born 1221), was stricken with a grave illness when he was an infant. His mother prayed to St. Francis of Assisi who, according to the account, not only cured the child but foretold his future greatness. "*O Buona Fortuna!* (O Good Fortune), cried the mother, in sheer gratitude. Thus, the child was renamed Bonaventure. He became known as the "Seraphic Doctor" and ultimately, St. Bonaventure. ***"Man proposes, God disposes."*** This oft-repeated phrase first appeared in Thomas á Kempis book, *The Imitation of Christ* (*Homo proponit, sed Deus disponit*). ***"Ask and it will be given to you; seek and you will find; knock and the door will be opened to you"*** (Mattthew 7:7).

We are blessed by Providence when we put ourselves in a situation to receive it. In order to hear the music, we must first turn the radio on. Providential assistance is always available. It is up to us to cooperate with its benefits. Finally, in order to find answers to some of the vexing problems associated with divine Providence, one may read Rev. Garrigou-Lagrange, OP's excellent work, *Providence*: God's loving care for man and the need for confidence in Almighty God.

St. Bonaventure, pray for us.

# Does Life Have Any Meaning?

W. Somerset Maugham was among the most popular writers of his era and reputedly the highest-paid author during the 1930-40s. His most popular novel, *The Razor's Edge* (1944) and made into a most successful movie two years later, is about the search for meaning. It takes as its theme the Zen Buddhist notion that the passage to enlightenment is narrow and painful. The path to enlightenment, therefore, is as narrow and sharp as a razor's edge. This bears an interesting contrast with Christ's statement concerning the "narrow path" (Matthew 7:13-14).

The protagonist, Larry Darrell, cannot abide the self-centered people who surround him and is driven to find a meaning to life other than the pursuit of money and material comfort. His odyssey takes him to India where he is mentored by a guru. He finds meaning in "goodness" although, by the end of the novel, his search is far from over.

Maugham's own personal search for meaning was not as illuminating. He was torn between his own search for meaning and his atheism. In the final year of his life (1965) he became terrified of dying and possibly being judged by a just and holy God. His life, he admitted, was one of debauchery and decadence. On his deathbed, he was losing his faith in secularism and tortured by the possibility that God exists. He summoned the famous atheist philosopher Alfred Ayer to his deathbed and begged for reassurance that he was on the brink of oblivion and not divine judgment. ***"Don't worry old boy,"*** Ayer said to him, ***"God does not exist and you will have no suffering in the afterlife."*** Nonetheless, oblivion is not a state in which anyone can find comfort.

In his biography, *The Summing Up*, Maugham alludes to what he believed to be the contradiction that all life poses.

> ***To myself I am the most important person in the world; though I do not forget that, not even taking into consideration so grand a concept of the absolute, I am of no consequence to the universe if I had never existed."***

How does one reconcile pride with common sense? Maugham was unable to reconcile a subjective perspective (I am all important) with an objective one (I am of no importance). Life, therefore, is a contradiction. But is it? Maugham's atheism prevented him from understanding the harmony that can exist between these two perspectives.

If God exists, then He, not I, is the center of reality. Furthermore, if God is a loving being, He is a transcendent subjectivity to which my subjectivity and that of each and every other human subjectivity are related. Therefore, from a subjective perspective, I am important and have meaning because I am related to God as subjectivity to Subjectivity. From the perspective of objectivity, I am important and have meaning because I am related to that which is the center of the universe. In this framework, I can avoid pride (I am the most important person in the world) and despair (I am of no importance whatsoever).

Maugham had the extreme misfortune of losing both his parents before he was ten years of age and then raised by a cold-hearted uncle. Despite his extraordinary powers of perception, Maugham failed to discover the meaning of his own life, though his was haunted by the possibility that his atheism might be wrong. He did not do himself any favors by summoning an atheist to his deathbed. Jacques Maritain would have brought a different message to the dying novelist. In *Existence and the Existent*, the Peasant of the Garonne writes,

> *"It is only from above that the antinomy can be resolved. If God exists, then not I, but He is the centre, and this time not in relation to a certain perspective . . . but speaking absolutely, and as transcendent subjectivity to which all subjectivities are referred."*

These words may reflect a philosophy that might be difficult for many to grasp. A more appropriate message is that God is both loving and forgiving. Salvation may be just a hairbreadth away.

In *The Razor's Edge*, Larry Darrell meets an anxiety ridden "unfrocked priest" who was terrified of God's mercy. Perhaps this fallen priest was Somerset Maugham in disguise. A fall from grace and a fear of judgment can be a formidable, even lethal, combination. Ultimately, the search for meaning is a wild goose chase if God is not in the picture. God maps out our meaning. Our search for meaning is really our search for God.

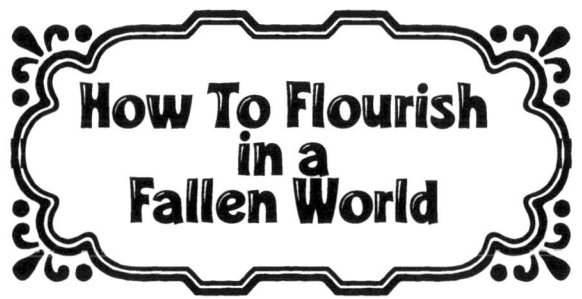

# How To Flourish in a Fallen World

For many people, the notion of "flourishing" seems a bit ambitious, if not idealistic. Some are merely trying to survive, while others are struggling to make both ends meet. Nonetheless, if Christians are called to become saints, it does not seem unrealistic to invite people to flourish in their personal lives. John the Evangelist tells us that Christ *"came that they may have life, and have it abundantly"* (John 10:10). Cardinal Sarah does not hesitate to employ the word, "flourish". In his 2019 book, *The Day Is Now Far Spent*, he bemoans the fact that many have rejected *"God, who ought to be the treasure and source of all human flourishing"*(224). He states that

> *Our humanity attains the fullness of flourishing, by accepting the gift of its sexed nature, while cultivating and developing it (160).*

And, he adds,

> *It is of capital importance here to rediscover the notion of human nature as the condition for the flourishing of freedom (158).*

I have organized a 5-step program that may be of help to

those who do not want to be another casualty in this fallen world, and hope for achieving a better and more productive state of life. What I propose is more in line with destiny than a world of dreams.

1) **Inspection:** The counterpart for inspection in medicine is "diagnosis"; in the world of "academe" it is examination; with regard to the computer it is "scanning". One surveys the landscape, so to speak, with the purpose of evaluating what it finds. Inspection should proceed with an open mind, but not one so open that it does not see anything that is worth knowing. The open mind should not be agnostic.

2) **Identification:** Here, we come to recognize bad ideas and distinguish them from good ideas. The former are destructive; the latter are beneficial. Bad ideas are not purely bad. They are deficient, or incomplete, lacking in wholeness and therefore unrealistic. A few examples: pleasure without conscience, choice without direction, will without reason, and power without restraint. By contrast, good ideas are complete, including goodness, truth, freedom, and justice.

3) **Isolation:** Having recognized the bad ideas, we should isolate them so that they do not harm us. This activity is comparable with what the computer does when it isolates a virus, or when it "uninstalls" a virus. It is also comparable with how our immune system works when it recognizes invading substances that are a threat to our health. Isolating bad ideas is like exiling them to where they can do no harm

4) **Inclusion:** Having recognized the good ideas, we must affirm them. They are the ideas that are required to make any progress toward a better life. Here, Johnny Mercer's lyrics to a 1940's tune are instructive:

*You've got to accentuate the positive,*

*eliminate the negative.*
*Latch on to the affirmative*
*and don't mess with Mister In-Between.*

We should not allow a bad idea to be mixed in with a good idea. Good ideas to not brook compromise.

5) **Incorporation:** It is not enough to identify and affirm good ideas. They must be fully incorporated into our life. This is accomplished by intelligence and virtue. Intelligence gives us light; virtue gives us strength. We cannot flourish if we do not see things correctly or lack the virtues that keep us strong and bind us to the needs of others. Good ideas lead to good actions and who can underestimate that value of a good action. As Shakespeare states in *The Merchant of Venice*, *"How far that little candle throws his beams! So shines a good deed in a naughty world"*.

Turning a bad idea into a principle can be devastating. Progress is a bad idea if it does not point to the right end. G. K. Chesterton has pointed out that,

> *As enunciated today, "progress" is simply a comparative of which we have not settled the superlative.*

In particular, the belief in today's society is that progress is the removal of inconvenience. But when the last inconvenience is removed from life, there is nothing left to give it substance. The belief was once held that a bird would fly at maximum speed in a resistanceless environment. The truth of the matter is that without the resisting air, the bird would have nothing against which to flap its wings and therefore could not fly at all. The complete absence of inconvenience is a condition of death.

St. Rose of Lima relates having received from God, the

message that true joy (the consequence of "flourishing") can be achieved only through conforming our lives to Christ's suffering on the Cross:

> *This is the only true stairway to paradise and without the Cross they can find no road to climb to heaven.*
>
> *"Do you not see, wrote the poet John Keats, "how necessary a world of pains and troubles is to school an intelligence and make it a soul?"*

We can flourish only if we first overcome the inevitable obstacles.

Equally devastating is removing a good idea because it is misinterpreted as a bad idea. A Canadian philosopher has stated that

> *Marriage is an archaic institution that has lost its moral force. But if we wish to provide a healthy, loving environment in which to reproduce our species, we'd better think up something quick to replace it.*

Marriage, however, is not only a good idea, but it is irreplaceable. There are no ready replacements for this divinely instituted arrangement. Without marriage, society loses its very foundation. In this case, a good idea is not replaced by another good idea, but with no idea at all. When we reject tradition, we reject, at the same time, the future on which it necessary depends.

Writing for the *American Psychologist*, authors Louise B. Silverstein and Carl F. Auerbach argue that fatherhood is not a good idea. In *Deconstructing the Essential Father*, they

> *see the argument that fathers are essential as an*

*attempt to reinstate male dominance by restoring the dominance of the traditional nuclear family with its contrasting masculine and feminine roles.*

The authors erroneously believe that fatherhood is a bad idea. But again, like marriage, fatherhood is irreplaceable. To misinterpret a good idea as a bad idea and replace it with nothing is a formula for social disaster. Saint John Paul II has stated that Original Sin is "above all" an attempt *"to abolish fatherhood"*. Unfortunately, there are many who believe that God is a bad idea. Nihilism, however, is never nourishing. And it is certainly better to flourish than to perish.

# Baseball and Life's Pilgrimage

Former baseball owner, Bill Veeck, is probably best known for sending a midget up to the plate as a pinch hitter, much to the wrath of the commissioner. Veeck was an eccentric promoter of the game, but he did have a clear sense of baseball's metaphysical significance. One poetic line he penned endears him to me forever:

> ***That's the true harbinger of Spring, not crocuses or swallows returning to Capistrano, but the sound of a bat on a ball.***

There was the Big Bang that set the universe in motion. And then there was the crack of the bat that set the baseball season in motion and sent millions of kids running off to baseball fields.

George F. Will, better known as a Pulitzer Prize winning political journalist, also understood and wrote about the transcendent importance of baseball. He was a serious candidate for the major league's commissioner and has authored two best-selling books on the game. For him, along with Veeck and innumerable others, the crack of the bat echoes the sound of creation.

Consider the following sample of Will's eloquent prose which appeared in a 1986 article entitled, *Louisville Slugger Sure Sign of a Higher Power*. A medieval philosopher could not have said it better:

*When Thomas Aquinas was ginning up proofs of God's existence, he neglected to mention the ash tree. It is the source of the Louisville slugger, and hence is conclusive evidence that a kindly mind superintends the universe. The Big Bang got the universe rolling and produced among the celestial clutter one planet, Earth, enveloped in an atmosphere that causes rain to patter on Pennsylvania ridgetops where ash trees grow. They grow surrounded by other trees that protect the ash trees from wind and force them to grow straight toward sunlight. The result is wood with the perfect strength required for the musical 'crack' that is the sound the cosmos makes each spring when it clears its throat and says, "We made it.*

In baseball jargon, "big bang" is a synonym for a homerun. As a footnote, Bernard Malamud, whose baseball novel, *The Natural* was adapted into a movie starring Robert Redford, asserted that *"The whole history of baseball has the quality of my theology"*.

Baseball's relationship with the universe is intriguing. Unlike in any other sport, foul balls are in play unless they land in the stands. If there were no stands, the field of play would extend through 360 degrees without limit. And a tie game, theoretically, could last forever. Baseball is richly suggestive of the universe set in the context of eternity. Baseball is man's favorite past-time as well as his favorite pastime. Its vectors reach out in every direction.

Hall of Fame great Rogers Hornsby may be forgiven for his over-estimation of baseball's importance. When asked what he did in the winter when there is no baseball, he responded by saying, *"I stare out the window and wait for spring."*

Baseball can get into a person's blood. Babe Ruth called it *"the only game"*. Excessive praise, however, does not diminish baseball's true importance. *"Baseball is something more than a game to an American boy,"* said former commissioner Judge Kenesaw Landis, *"it is his training field for life work."* And President Herbert Hoover maintained that *"Next to religion, baseball has furnished a greater impact on American life than any other institution"*.

If a youngster cannot fulfill his ambition of being a major league baseball player, he might have to settle for being President of the United States. When he was a young lad in Kansas, Dwight David Eisenhower and a friend went fishing together and shared their dreams. The former hoped to become a major league ballplayer, while the latter confessed his dream of becoming President of the United States. Neither of them got their wish.

Baseball sets the context for a pilgrimage. It is rightly called "base-ball" because it represents a progression from one base to another. Hence, the order of first, second, and third base. Would that our lives could develop in accord with the right order. But, significantly, there is no fourth base. After third, there is "home" were the progress of the pilgrim is completed. Home is suggestive of heaven, the reward for a faithful advance in virtue. The great sin in the game of baseball is to die on third. It is not good enough to be close, but only to complete the circuit. Reaching third does not count on the score board. Reaching home is all that counts.

This distinctive nomenclature raises the question, where is the batter before he reaches first base? He is not "home" as yet, since he did not complete his journey around the bases. He stands at the plate, like all of us, as an exile. He is really no place. His initial aspiration is to get on base. He is the pilgrim who wants to progress, and fears that his failure will dispatch him to the dugout, a kind of Hades for failures.

Symbolically, baseball is a re-enactment of Dante's Divine Comedy. The great poet begins as an exile and has to pass through the Inferno and Purgatory before he can reach Paradise. "In the midway at this our mortal life, I found me in a gloomy wood, astray, gone from the path direct" (Cary translation). This is how Dante finds himself, speaking for all of mankind, at the beginning of his masterpiece. And so, we find the pilgrim at the plate eager to find his direction and to continue a journey that will give his existence meaning.

Baseball, of course, is not exactly the same as life, but it symbolizes it. Its essential importance is to remind us of what life should be: a pilgrimage according to a prescribed order that requires a host of virtues, including faith, courage, loyalty, discipline, hard work, and a commitment to fair play.

# Open to Everything, Dedicated to Nothing

Wrote G.K. Chesterton:

*Merely having an open mind is nothing," "The object of opening the mind, as of opening the mouth, is to shut it again on something solid.*

We have elevated "openness" to the status of a principle and in the process have forgotten what it is that we should select. Therefore, we are left hungry. Political correctness, the attempt to please everyone, is a restaurant without a menu, a church without dogma, a life without purpose. When we are open to everything, we find ourselves dedicated to nothing.

Fulton J. Sheen explains, in his monumental work, *Life of Christ* (1958), the essential dynamism of the Catholic Church which holds it together and gives it both meaning and unity. He refers to a delicate balance between two forces, one seeking the center, the other going out to the world:

*As unity in doctrine and authority is the centripetal force which keeps the life of the Church one, catholicity is the centrifugal force which enables her to expand and absorb redeemed humanity without distinction of race or color.*

The Church reaches out, but she has something to offer. Her teaching is not sterile; her outreach is not empty. In a sense, she provides food for all.

St. Jerome's University, in Waterloo. ON, purportedly a Catholic institution, has decided to fly the LGBTQ flag on its campus to celebrate "Pride" month. Interim President Scott Kline, whose term began on July I, 2019, defended the action as a way of sending the message that "all are welcome in this place". The immediate reaction to the move has shown significant evidence of outrage and division. Catholics do not believe that we can serve God and mammon at the same time or that a house divided against itself can continue to stand (Matthew 12:22-28).

Dr. Kline is enthusiastic about being open, even when it is closed to what is essential. He is an apostle of the centrifugal. But in this case, the centrifugal is like the receding galaxies. Everyone is invited to the meal, but there is no food on the plate.

It is an odd thing for a university to "welcome" everyone since not everyone who applies is admitted. Sexual life-style does not qualify anyone for admission. Therefore, those who are not admitted are not welcomed "in this place". "Welcome" is a politically correct buzzword that is intended to make everyone feel comfortable. But in the world of academe, rejection, firings, dismissals, and failures, are a daily occurrence.

I taught at SJU for 32 years. Logic was the one subject I taught most often. I recall explaining the *"fallacy of accent"* to my students. I used the example of *"Today the captain is sober,"* which places the accent on "today" and suggests that the captain is not sober on other days. In selecting the LGBTQ consortium to offer a sign of welcome may lead one to infer that other groups are not welcome. What about that much maligned group that identifies itself as "pro-life"? Where is their flag? And what about plumbers, carpenters, masons, handy-men, and construction workers? To single out one group and reject all the rest does not serve the purpose of welcoming everyone. If Dr. Kline welcomes all groups, he should be just as willing to fly the flag of the Ku Klux Klan. He would not do this for the simple reason that he does not believe in what he says. Hoisting the LGBTQ flag is a capitulation to a fashion. The Klan is not fashionable these days.

The Catholic Church teaches that it is an insult to anyone to be identified according to his sexual preference. Such a labeling can serve as a stigma. Being called "illegitimate," thankfully, is a stigma that we have pretty much expelled from our day-to-day conversation. The Church's *Pastoral Care of Homosexuals* states the following (sec.16):

> *The human person, made in the image and likeness of God, can hardly be adequately described by a reductionist reference to his or her sexual orientation. . . . Today the church provides a badly needed context for the care of the human person when she refuses to consider the person as a 'heterosexual' or a 'homosexual' and insists that every person has a fundamental identity: the creature of God and, by grace, his child and heir to eternal*

*life.*

The Church welcomes sinners, but only because she is confident, given the possibility of grace and forgiveness, that being a sinner is not a permanent condition. The Church welcomes everyone, but she does not have admission requirements.

Dr. Kline has made an egregious misstep which is not only inconsistent with Catholic tradition, but with common sense. Whether he realizes it or not, he is giving approval to life-styles that are injurious to families and incompatible with so fundamental a value as personal health. Does he welcome a plague of sexually transmitted diseases? He has brought disgrace to a long-standing Catholic institution. By his own actions, he appears to be more committed to fads than to Catholic teaching.

From a personal point of view, Dr. Kline has made it clear to me that I am not welcomed on the SJU campus. After more than three decades of diligent teaching, I am now, and fo

# The Power of For

One of the most agreeable phrases in the English language is, "This is for you". A certain brewery has capitalized on the expression with the words, "This Bud's for you". A most welcomed phrase for me is "There is mail for you". It brings to mind that the entire postal system is dedicated to delivering, often from great distances, something that belongs to me. Federal laws ensure that my name as the addressee is honored and protected.

A Jewish scholar (Professor Lapide) has pointed out that in Aramaic, the language in which Jesus spoke, the command to love God relates to the accusative case, whereas love of neighbor relates to the dative. In other words, our love of God is direct while we are for our neighbor. We do not apply the corporal works of mercy to God since He does not need them. But we are for our neighbor in the sense of ministering to his needs as a doctor uses medicine for his patients.

Gifts are usually well received and they also serve the benefactor well. We are beings who are made to give and are happiest when we give from the heart. One of the greatest of all gifts is provided by nature and comes free of charge. Though it does come from the heart, we can say, sadly, that it is often spurned for something of lesser value.

Mechthild of Magdeburg, a thirteenth century mystic, relates a vision she had concerning the milk of the Madonna. In her description of the breastfeeding Christ Child, she writes,

> *Then the sweet milk flowed from her pure heart painlessly, and the child suckled his food in human wise.*

According to the physiology of her time, breast feeding was seen as a gift of heart. This is an instance in which natural human intuition has something more profound to say than what we find in biology text books. Oliver Wendell Holmes understood how nature on its own can be more provident than the brainiest of scientists. Accordingly, he once said,

> *A pair of substantial mammary glands has the advantage over the two hemispheres of the most learned professor's brain in the art of compounding a nutritive fluid for infants.*

Nature has a bounty for which technology has no adequate substitute.

The universal connotations of mother's milk flowing from a center of human charity and generosity are perhaps most  famously expressed in Shakespeare's metaphor, "the milk of human kindness". Mother's milk is symbolic of a host of natural human virtues. In addition to love, generosity, and kindness, it also includes fidelity, dedication, and hope. These are virtues that have no expiration date.

When St. Augustine said of Mary that *"She gave milk to our bread,"* he was referring to how her milk enriches the body of Christ and consequently, the Eucharist. In a scientific sense, she fortified the Eucharist with Vitamin D. Her milk, then, is an unbroken stream flowing from the Madonna to her Child, to the Eucharist, and finally to all communicants. Her milk, therefore, is "for" everyone. Mary feeds us, though indirectly, with the milk of her own kindness. The Eucharist may be richer than we think.

While hanging on the cross, Christ prayed from the twenty-second Psalm, *"My God, My God, why hast Thou forsaken me?"* That same Psalm contains the words,

*Thou indeed did bring me forth from the womb;*
*Thou gave me confidence upon my mother's breast.*

At this moment, the beginning and the end of temporal life were brought together.

Breast feeding can be seen as an act of charity. But in addition to this, it is an act of justice, for the mother's milk belongs to the baby. In other words, the milk is for the baby. The mother, herself, has no particular use for her own milk. It provides her child with nourishment and warmth. It also strengthens the child's immune system so that it can be better protected from infection and disease. Moreover, the mother's milk arrives fortuitously at the time of childbirth when feeding her hungry infant is most propitious.

Breast feeding is the inauguration of the face-to-face relationship. The newborn's eyes have a natural affinity for the mother's face to which the infant is spontaneously attracted. Reciprocally, the mother lowers her head as she looks down to her child to establish visual contact. It is love at first sight, a love that needs to be firmly grounded and repeatedly drawn from in order to deal with all the problems that may arise over the years between the mother and her growing child. The benefits of breast feeding do not represent a mere complementary relationship between mother and child. They prepare and strengthens both mother and child for all subsequent interpersonal relationships.

The demonstrable fact that the milk belongs to the baby establishes the truth that a human being is not an isolated entity riveted to its own selfish needs. The mother is for the child, just as Adam, from whose side Eve was taken, is for his wife, and Christ on the Cross, from whose side gushed blood and water, is for all other human beings. We can say, then, that the husband is for the wife, the mother is for her baby, and the family is for society. Everything about Christianity resonates with the unprepossessing preposition, for. The power of for is fortuitous, formative, formidable, and forward-thinking. We might say that the power of for has the potential to unify the world.

Writing is primarily for the reader, and certainly not for self-aggrandizement. So, too, in the same sense, teaching is for the student, just as parenting is for the child, and nursing is for the patient. Saint Thomas Aquinas taught that the end of the work supersedes the end of the worker. Therefore, the doctor should be more concerned about the health of his patients than his own remunerations.

Jean-Paul Sartre could not have been more wrong when he redefined the human being as a "Being-for-itself" (*être-pour-soi*). We are beings for others, as testified by the mother breast feeding her young.

The secular world teaches us to think of peace and justice in socio-economic terms. But is there a better place to begin the movement toward peace and justice than with the mother breast feeding her child in a face-to-face, I-Thou relationship?

# Meditation on a Peach Stone

I began my breakfast one morning in recent memory with a peach, one that had reached its zenith of ripeness. Succulent, juicy, and pleasing to the palate, its consumption was an auspicious way to inaugurate the day. But, on further inspection, this tasty globe of fruit fell short of perfection. A stone, hidden in the center, warned me to be careful. I did not want to chip a tooth. Why must this stony inconvenience be part of an otherwise splendid morsel? Not completely satisfied with this gustatory delight, I began thinking about the arrival of stone-less peaches sometime in the future.

We now have seedless grapes, seedless apples, and seedless watermelons. One pundit has welcomed the future watermelon in a rind-less form. We even have wingless chickens (convenient for the consumer, but not for the chicken). The march of progress, I thought, should include the peach.

It was early in the morning and my philosophical sensibilities had not yet awakened. Suppose, I then thought, that rather than quibble about the stone and discard it, I planted it. In time, and with proper care, a peach tree would emerge displaying innumerable peaches, each possessing a seed-containing stone of its own. Authorities on the subject inform me that a standard peach tree grows to 10 to 15 feet high and can yield 6 to 8 bushels of peaches per year. Now if we planted the seeds of each of these mouth-watering delectables, we would have an orchard. And if we continued the process, we would, in just a few generations, have enough peaches to feed everyone in the world.

The peach stone is an inconvenience; it is, however, at least in its potentiality, a cornucopia, a treasure trove, a bonanza, a food bank, and a never ending gift to posterity. The biological origin of the more than 6 billion people that now populate the world had its origin in the single zygote of our primal parents, a cell no larger than a grain of sugar.

Saint Thomas Aquinas writes, in his *Summa Theologica* (III, 60,1) about things of nature containing a "certain hidden sanctity" or a "sacred secret" (*sacrum secretum*). When we falsely interpret the peach-stone as an inconvenience, we fail to appreciate its prodigious secret, one that God has inserted as a reward for the perspicacious. For Aquinas, nature is a window to the Eternal Law, revealing something of the mind of God. To modify a citation from G. K. Chesterton,

> *If a peach-stone can grow into a tree that provides nourishment for human beings, what might not the heart of man become in its long journey to the stars?*

I prefer to speak of the peach-stone as the peach's "core," a word derived from the Latin *cor*, referring to the "heart". This delicate morsel, we can say, has a "heart". Blessed Cardinal Newman's famous motto is *"cor ad cor loquitur"* (Heart speaking to heart). Suddenly, I viewed the peach as a microcosm of myself, equipped with a fleshly exterior and a hidden heart. Its heart, like the hearts of humans, can touch others and enliven them, as Christ did for his apostles, and disciples, and all who encountered him. The heart can bring things to life, and so too, the heart of a peach. The peach stone is really a seed-protecting tabernacle.

My morning delicacy not only contained seeds of prodigious potentiality, but a moral lesson for all of us. There are times when what appears to be an inconvenience turns out to be a blessing. As G. K. Chesterton has reminded us,

> *An inconvenience is only an adventure wrongly considered; an adventure is an inconvenience rightly considered.*

If we could somehow remove all inconveniences from our lives, we would have, in the same process, removed everything that makes life meaningful. Real progress is seeing the value of inconvenience and capitalizing on it. When the baby cries out in the middle of the night, a terrible nocturnal inconvenience for sound asleep parents, he is opening the door to hugs that are mutually humanizing. The ordeal of training for an athletic event is a way of gaining strength and overall fitness. When the moth struggles to free itself from the cocoon, it is drying itself so that it is able to fly. According to a charming fable, birds were once wingless. When God gifted them with wings, they complained about this cumbersome inconvenience and demanded their removal. But God told them that if they only lifted their burden, they could fly. Burdens need not be stumbling blocks, they can get us airborne.

We wonder how convenient certain conveniences really are. Fast-food drive-thrus are built for convenience. A recent study, however, reports that 70% of drivers who went inside to get their coffee did so in shorter time than those who went through the drive-thru. Remaining in the idling car, in addition to contributing to pollution, is more inconvenient in terms of time, than doing a bit of leg work (which is good for one's health). The convenience lies in not getting out of the car, a dubious convenience since it comes at the price of causing several attendant inconveniences. The drive-thru is not a friend of environmentalists and not encouraged by health professionals. It also minimizes social interaction.

The TV remote, the jet plane, the micro-wave oven, the clip-on tie, I-pads, computers, and wash-and-wear clothes all represent victories over inconvenience. But these victories should not form a philosophy. The peach-stone tells us otherwise. Let us not be misled. Inconvenience itself is not an ideal. Certain inconveniences are really work-orders from God. It behooves us to recognize them as such and to put them into practice. At any rate, eating a peach is food for thought.

# With All Your Faults I Love You Still

The Good Book, which makes no concession to political correctness while conveying a message that survives the test of time, tells us that *"Where there is no vision, the people perish"* (Proverbs 29:18). In this respect, it differs radically, from the daily newspaper. The difference between these two sources of information may be compared with the difference between eyesight and vision. The roots of eyesight are in the optic nerve. One sees what is going on in the moment. The roots of vision are in the heart. The heart sees what the eye cannot see. It focuses on something grander, something good that has not yet come into being.

A nation must have a vision in order to survive. Without a unifying vision, people are let loose, like pearls from their unifying string, and become aimless wanderers, desperately trying to have their own way and warring desperately against each other. A nation's vision is exemplified by its flag. The flag of the United States of America symbolizes the notion that all its citizens are Americans and are entitled to all the rights and privileges for which that country stands. It conveys a unifying message, one that arises not from something reported in a newspaper, but from a vision shared by all who come together to seek a better life and live in harmony as one nation. We must return to civics 101: *"Where there is no flag, the people perish"*.

 Drew Brees is one of the NFL's outstanding quarterbacks. In 2010, he led his New Orleans Saint to their first Super Bowl championship by a 31-17 victory over the Indianapolis Colts, and was named the Most Valuable Player. Brees is known for his extensive charity work in New Orleans. Recently, he and his wife contributed $5 million of their own money to assist victims of the Covid-19 virus. All this was set aside, however, when he stated that he *"will never agree with anybody disrespecting the flag of the United States of America or our country."*

We are currently suffering from acute short-sightedness and can lay a great deal of blame for this sorry condition on the Media. Distinguished historian David McCullough avers that "The study of history is an antidote to the hubris of the present – the idea that everything we have, everything we do, and everything we think is the ultimate, the best." Former US President Woodrow Wilson was on the mark when he said that "The flag is the embodiment, not of sentiment, but of history. Respect for the flag is timeless and unassailable.

Brees was royally abused for his statement. NBA analyst Charles Barkley opined on the matter:

> *It was insensitive, especially during this time, but I thought the negative reaction was overkill. I've never heard a bad word about Drew Brees*

*in my life. He made a mistake but we've got to a point in society where everybody in social media thinks they are God, judge, and jury.*

Under a barrage of criticism, Brees apologized. He did have a supporter, however: the President of the United States:

*[Brees] should not have taken back his original stance on honoring the flag, our magnificent American flag. Old Glory is to be revered, cherished, and flown high.*

President Trump would have happily endorsed the lyrics penned by Ira Gershwin in 1931 for his brother's tribute to the flag, *Of Thee I Sing*:

*Shining Star and Inspiration*
*Worthy of a Mighty Nation.*

The American banner has weathered many storms and, in the immortal words of Francis Scott Key, *"The flag is still there"*.  In August of 1925, 60,000 members of the Ku Klux Klan, with the approval of D.C. officials, marched to the white House to display their ever-increasing numbers across America. As the New York Sun reported,

*The Klan put it all over its enemies. The parade was grander and gaudier, by far than anything the wizards had prophesied. It was larger, it was thicker, it was higher in tone.*

At that time there were between 3 and 5 million Klan members. This was, indeed, a most disconcerting spectacle, but the flag continued to wave. In 1963 five times as many people crowded Washington, D.C. and listened in rapture to Rev. Martin Luther King, Jr's *I Have A Dream*. King had not lost sight of either the flag or the vision.

Historian Shelby Foote, an authority on the Civil War, pointed out that before the skirmish, people said, *"the United States are,"* emphasizing state independence. After the way, it became *"the United States is"*. *"And that sums up what the war accomplished,"* according to Foote, *"It made us an 'is'."*

A great deal of blood has been spilled to make the United States united. The flag bears testimony to that fact. It is what has endured when so many other things have faded into oblivion.

The flag is not a witness to current atrocities. It is a shining hope that things will not always be this way. Love is both accepting as well as forgiving. *"With all your faults, I love you still,"* from *It Had to Be You*, by Isham Jones and lyricist Gus Kahn, represents the heart of any true lover. No one, no thing, and no country is perfect. If we waited until perfection arrived, no one would ever love, no one would ever be loved, and the world would descend into an abyss of permanent misery.

Robert E. Lee has been much maligned in recent years. In 2017, Governor Andrew Cuomo, who does not think that there is any place in his state for pro-lifers, had the distinguished general and educator's bust removed from The Hall of Fame for Great Americans, situated on the grounds of Bronx Community College. Nonetheless, like Drew Brees, the honorable general had something to say that is worth reiterating and even taken to heart:

> ***The march of Providence is so slow and our own desires so impatient; the work of progress is so immense and our means of aiding it so feeble; the life of humanity is so long, that of the individual so brief, that we often see only the ebb of the advancing wave and are thus discouraged. It is history that teaches us to hope.***

ConFLAGration

19  20

20  20

# AMERICA

THIS TREE MUST COME DOWN

FOR THE EXCLUSIVE USE OF "THE PERSECUTED."

# Monumental Principles

The Know Nothing Party, originally known as the American Party, came into prominence in 1853. Party members supported the deportation of beggars and criminals, a 21-year naturalization period for all immigrants, and the elimination of all Catholics from public office. It was a secret society, with secret passwords and hand signs. Members were not allowed to talk about their society and when asked about it, they would reply, "I know nothing," hence their name. At the height of its power, in the 1850's, the Party claimed more than 100 elected congressmen, eight governors, a controlling share of half-a dozen state legislatures from Massachusetts to California, and thousands of local politicians.

Between 1845 and 1854, some 2.9 million immigrants poured into the country, many of them Catholic. The intensely xenophobic Know Nothing Party went into action. Posters in the Boston area proclaimed:

*All Catholics and all persons who favor the Catholic Church are . . . vile imposters, liars, villains, and cowardly cutthroats.*

Churches were burned and Know Nothing gangs spread to a number of major cities including Boston, New York, Philadelphia, New Orleans, St. Louis, and San Francisco. Lincoln's commitment to the Declaration of Independence and the Gettysburg Address, however, prevailed.

> *As a nation,"* Lincoln declared, *"we began by declaring that 'all men are created equal.' We now practically read it 'all men are created equal, except negroes.' When the Know-Nothings get control, it will read 'all men are created equal, except Negroes, and foreigners, and Catholics.' When it comes to this I should prefer emigrating to some country where they make no pretense of loving liberty — to Russia, for instance, where despotism can be taken pure, and without the base alloy of hypocrisy.*

Lincoln knew exactly what the Know Nothings were up to and stood firmly in their way.

America is now besieged by a nameless group that is striking against the very principles of freedom and human rights for which her greatest president fought and died. On July 3, 2020, President Trump delivered his most patriotic speech in the shadows of Mount Rushmore, in South Dakota where Lincoln's image, along with those of George Washington, Thomas Jefferson, and Theodore Roosevelt, are carved in stone. At the same time, this same nameless group was demeaning these four titanic figures as representing "White Supremacy". History tends to repeat itself, though names may change. But history also teaches us hope. America is extraordinarily resilient. The Know-Nothing secret society is no longer with us although it has re-surfaced in various guises from the Ku Klux Klan to Planned Parenthood. Remnants of it may have metamorphosed into the plague against which America is now defending itself.

The President made it clear that the figures carved in Mt. Rushmore stand for the founding spirit of America which is also its lasting legacy:

> *Today, we pay tribute to the exceptional lives and extraordinary legacies of George Washington, Thomas Jefferson, Abraham Lincoln, and Teddy Roosevelt. I am here as your President to proclaim before the country and before the world: This monument will never be desecrated these heroes will never be defaced, their legacy will never, ever be destroyed, their achievements will never be forgotten, and Mount Rushmore will stand forever as an eternal tribute to our forefathers and to our freedom.*

On that same occasion, Kristi Noem, governor of South Dakota, strongly advised Americans not to forget her Founding Fathers. People are *"paralyzed by the present and defeated about the future,"* she said. But rather than destroy history, she encouraged people to learn from it.

Gutzon Borglum is a name that is familiar to very few American, but the presidential faces he carved on Mt. Rushmore is something that they are not likely to forget. The lifelike figures of Washington, Jefferson, Theodore Roosevelt, and Lincoln stand 60 feet tall from a mountain height of 5,725 feet high and can be observed from miles away. The project required the assistance of 400 workers and the blasting away of 450,000  short tons of rock. Granite was the canvas and dynamite was the chisel. It took a dozen years, from 1927-1939, for Borglum and his assistants to complete the work. The more than two million tourists who visit the site in the Black Hills of South Dakota annually no doubt scratch their heads and think, "How on earth did human ingenuity manage carry out such a colossal project while compromising neither beauty nor accuracy?"

Borglum was fascinated with heroic nationalism (he named his only child, Lincoln) and creating artistic works on a gigantic scale. He chose Washington to be the most dominant figure. It was an appropriate way, according to his thinking, of incarnating the following words of America's first president:

> *The preservation of the sacred fire of Liberty, and the destiny of the Republican model of Government, are justly considered as deeply, perhaps as finally staked, on the experiment entrusted to the hands of the American people.*

Liberty was thus carved in stone. And no security guards would be needed, as they are at the Louvre, to prevent theft. For President Lincoln, liberty and democracy "shall not perish from the earth".

Like the Ten Commandments, the faces on Mt. Rushmore are immortalized in granite. As such, they symbolize a lasting tribute to liberty and human rights. If the presidents they personify were not perfect in life (and what mere human being is?), who, then, is without sin and morally justified in hurling the first stone? Once again, America must reinforce her principles of liberty and equality, and reaffirm its gratitude to the heroes who stood fast for these sacred values. If the bizarre rush to judgment on the part of the new Know Nothings were to be realized, everyone would be disgraced and no one would be left to guide America back to the greatness and prosperity she once enjoyed.

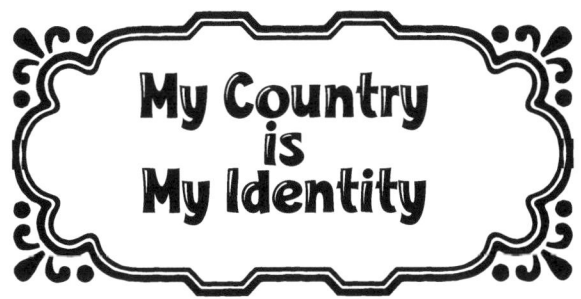

# My Country is My Identity

I am an individual, which is to say, the sum of all my idiosyncratic traits, inclinations, and unique accomplishments. I am also a person, which includes all my relationships with others including the long gone members of my family tree. When I say that I am an American, I contain the contributions of all my forefathers. I can be proud to be an American because I stand at the summit of her history, including the good as well as the bad. History, in ways that I may not understand, has formed me. I learn more about myself when I study American history.

Long ago when I was a high school student, I took a course in American History, which is different than studying the subject. Our teacher was a fine, upstanding gentleman, but he spent most of the classroom time kibitzing with a loquacious student who sat directly in front of his desk. I was hoping that he would finally say, "And now we will begin the class in American History".

So, I watched the clock, but did not pass the course with flying colors. I would have preferred the droning voice of Ben Stein who played an American history teacher in the 1986 movie, *Ferris Bueller's Day Off*.

American history is a most exciting subject. It would be a welcomed challenge for me to convince students of that fact. My chance came in my very first year of teaching. I was substituting for the regular teacher who was on sick leave. My assignment was to instruct a class of Junior High students in the thrilling adventure of the Spanish-American War. What could be more exciting: The Battles of San Juan Hill and Manila Bay, the Yellow Fever, the mysterious explosion of the *USS Maine*, the naval blockade of Cuba, and finally, in 1898, the Treaty of Paris?

Two weeks passed and I had failed to fuel my class with any degree of enthusiasm. In order to motivate them, I kept them after school and would release them only when they could correctly answer a question. I tried to make the questions easy, since I was also eager to get home. Finally, in order to free my last captive student, I asked her, "What two countries were involved in the Spanish-American War?" She looked at me sleepily and said, "I don't know". That was good enough for me. She really did not know.

Ralph Waldo Emerson described the beginning of the American Revolution in deathless imagery:

> **By the rude bridge that arched the flood,**
> **their flag unfurled to April's breeze,**
> **Here once the embattled farmers stood,**
> **and fired the shot heard round the world.**

That shot, however, did not resound in my students' ears. History, for them, was drudgery. Perhaps I should have entered my class dressed as a Minute Man.

We are, whether we realize it or not, historical creatures. Only the human being, among all animals, knows his grandparents. Only human beings keep a family tree. The past is a prologue to posterity. "To cut off history," writes psychotherapist Rollo May, "is to sever our arterial link with humanity." We have blood lines that flow from the past. "Breathes there a man with a soul so dead," wrote Sir Walter Scott, "Who never to himself hath said, This is my own my native land."

Piety may be a lost virtue. It is respect for parents, tradition, and country. It is a profound respect for all the forces that preceded us and brought us into being. A German wordsmith tried to restore its original meaning by giving it a new name: *Blutphlichtverbundenheit* (blood-duty-connectness). This elongated word did not catch on, but it does indicate in a clear way, the nature of piety. Before we ask the question, "Where am I going?" we should first ask the question, "Where did I come from?" Anniversaries, celebrations, commemorations, ceremonies, festivals, holidays, and feast days are all expressions of piety. Without this noble virtue, we are isolated on the time spectrum with neither past nor future. Nor is there anyone to whom we could offer thanks.

These are iconoclastic times, when they should be occasions for expressing gratitude to the great figures who came

before us. Our debt is large, but our memories are weak. William H. Marnell, a Harvard graduate, is the author of the highly acclaimed book, *The First Amendment*. In *The Good Life of Western Man* (1971), he pays homage to America's Founding Fathers.

> *The principle of duty and service to the state,"* he writes, *"has never found a finer, more intelligent, more dedicated expression than found in the American Founding Fathers, and the United States has never since been quite so mature as it was the hour it was born."*

That is high praise for the likes of Washington, Adams, Jefferson, Madison, Jay, Hamilton, and others, and strong criticism for the political leaders of the present.

> *Antiquity never saw exemplified in finer fashion,* he added, *the principle that the good life is the life of service to one's fellow man* (page 174).

When we think of the Founding Father of Christianity, we think of the blameless figure of Christ. The Church that He founded has continued for over 2,000 years. And yet, the statues, memories, images, and records of both the Founders of America and the Founder of Christianity are disrespected, desecrated, and dismissed! We recall the words of G. K. Chesterton in thinking about the rejection of Christianity:

> *I could not abandon the faith, without falling back on something more shallow than the faith. I could not cease to be a Catholic, except by becoming something more narrow than a Catholic.*

What does an American fall back on once she rejects the contributions of her Founding Fathers?

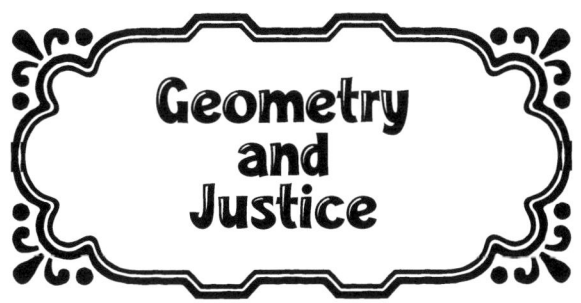

# Geometry and Justice

Geometry teaches us more than geometry. It supplies us with lessons that are actually indispensable for morality. A triangle is a three-sided two dimensional figure whose interior angles add up to 180 degrees. That is the definition of a triangle. An equilateral triangle has three equal sides, an isosceles triangle has two equal sides, and a scalene triangle has no equal sides. They are different, but they all conform to the definition of a triangle. No geometer would disagree. Engineering would not be possible if engineers began treating triangles as squares and squares as triangles. In this regard, there is peaceful conformity between all triangles and their unifying definition.

A human being is a rational creature endowed by God with unalienable dignity. It does not matter whether a human being is white, black, or brown, Christian, Jew, or Muslim. All these types correspond to the definition of a human being. It would be wrong to deny humanity to any of these types. Geometry, then, gives us a fundamental model of justice. If someone conforms to the definition of a human being, then, he is a human being. Justice has a kind of geometric quality in that it equalizes the particular with the universal, just as a scalene triangle, despite its three unequal sides, is still a triangle.

A square has four sides. Therefore, it does not qualify

as being a triangle. If a medical doctor is not interested in health, he cannot claim to be a medical doctor. Here, there is an unbridgeable discrepancy between what he does and what he claims to be. Likewise, if the home plate umpire is not concerned about the strike zone, he is not an umpire. And if a lawyer rejects justice, he disqualifies himself from being a lawyer.

Racism, which is universally deplored, is a species of prejudice. A person is said to be prejudicial when he negatively evaluates a person not in relation to that person but in relation to a group or class of which he is a member. Such an act is decidedly unfair. Therefore, prejudice is a species of injustice. Racism and prejudice are both examples of injustice.

In America's fight against racism, strangely enough, it ignores prejudices against Catholics. But one wonders if the fight against racism is pure if it is separated from a more general fight against all forms of prejudice. We would expect that lawyers, who commit themselves to defending justice, would be in the trenches fighting against all forms of injustice, including prejudice against Catholics. Unfortunately, this is not the case. In fact, in some circles, prejudice against Catholics is seen as politically acceptable and even career-advancing.

In late 2018, while evaluating the nomination of Brian Buescher to serve as a district judge in Nebraska, Kamala Harris posed a series of questions insinuating that his involvement in the Knights of Columbus disqualified him from serving on the bench (*National Review*, Alexandra Desanctis, Aug, 11, 2020 "Kamala Harris's Anti-Catholic Bigotry"). She asked him if he was *"aware that the Knights of Columbus opposed marriage equality when [he] joined the organization"* and whether he had *"ever, in any way, assisted with or con-*

*tributed to advocacy against women's reproductive rights."*

Following Harris, Democratic senator from Hawaii, Mazie Hirono, went a bit further, asking Buescher whether he intended to *"end [his] membership with this organization to avoid any appearance of bias"* — in other words, intimating that she would withhold her vote at least until he had left the Knights of Columbus. At the behest of Nebraska senator, Ben Sasse, Buescher was eventually confirmed. It is important to note that the Senate later voted unanimously to reaffirm the constitutional clause forbidding religious tests for public officeholders. But the fact remains that Harris was guilty of reprehensible anti-Catholic bigotry, and there's no reason to believe her views have changed. She is now Joe Biden's Vice-presidential running mate.

It is worth pointing out that the United States Supreme Court includes five Catholics. And it is clear from recent decisions that they do not think alike or vote in the same way. The notion that a Catholic is unfit to be a judge simply because he is a Catholic is a clear instance of injustice as well as prejudice. The more relevant question is whether a lawyer can call herself a lawyer if she is an enemy of justice? Newt Gingrich, former Speaker of the House has stated on Fox News that

> *The consequences of Harris' openly anti-Catholic bias will be felt as other anti-Catholics draw encouragement from her bigotry to increase the activism and intensity of their assaults on Catholic institutions and Catholic personalities.*

If a Catholic is a true Catholic, then he affirms that justice is not only a virtue, but a cardinal virtue along with prudence, fortitude, and wisdom. A true Catholic, then, precisely because he is Catholic, has a credential for being a judge. His appointment to the bench should be welcomed, not disqualified. Here we have, in the examples of Harris and Hirono,

two individuals who presume to be defenders of justice but are really its antagonists. Their conduct should ignite a national outrage. Nevertheless, in certain instances, justice continues to take a back seat to political correctness.

The fight against racism should be based on a fight against all forms of injustice. It remains forever than all triangles — equilateral, isosceles, scalene — are all equally triangles. It also remains forever that all human beings are human beings, notwithstanding their color, creed, or affiliation. If America fights injustice selectively, it has not begun the fight.

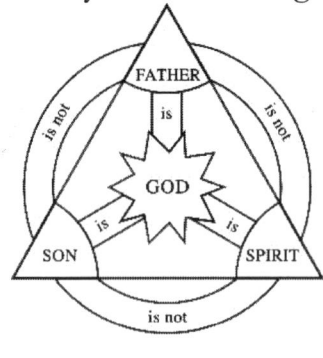

# Something Worse Than Racism

Racism is unquestionably an evil that all of us should endeavor to eliminate. And it is universally regarded as such. The great impediment to eradicating this evil is that many people do not understand the nature of racism. For example, a co-founder of Black Lives Matter has stated that

*White ppl [people] are recessive genetic defects. This is factual,"* and that *"white ppl [people] need white supremacy as a mechanism to protect their survival as a people because all they can do is produce themselves.*

Being white, or of any color, for that matter does not exemplify racism. The fact that such a statement receives a great deal of publicity is most disheartening and does nothing to eliminate racism.

Racism is an injustice that unfairly categorizes a person by a factor (color) that is entirely irrelevant. Because it is a  form of prejudice directed at an entire race of human beings, it has a much wider scope than prejudice inveighed against a particular person. Therefore, its evil is magnified. Woody Allen once quipped that he was banned from his high school's chess club because he was too short. While prejudice of any kind is not a laughing matter, Allen does offer a good example of an irrelevant factor determining a person's status.

Evil as racism is, there is something worse, something to which society, so it seems, is curiously indifferent. Color is a morally neutral category. One cannot judge another as good or bad simply because of color. The injustice here lies in the fact that something neutral is judged to be something defective. But suppose prejudice was directed at a person because he was doing something good. This would be worse than racism for it despises not something that is neutral but something that is good. Christ is the ultimate example of this kind of evil.

AND THEY LED HIM AWAY IN BONDS, AND GAVE HIM UP TO THE GOVERNOR, PONTIUS PILATE

Recently, a small Catholic school in Canada, one that has been cited by the Newman Society as a reliable and orthodox

Catholic center of learning, requested government funding for three of its students to do routine, but important work around the College. The request was denied because the school is pro-life and neither it nor its students can approve of a woman's "right" to abortion, an approval which the liberal government of Canada requires. The school's president informed the government that owing to its own integrity, it could not attest to something that it regarded as morally wrong. But the president also questioned how the government could violate Canada's *Charter of Rights* by refusing to honor a legitimate difference of opinion:

> ***For all the talk of Charter rights in the attestation, this program is remarkably obtuse about the ways in which this process subverts the religious rights enshrined in the Charter.***

The government is not the property of the liberal party. Rather, it should be the servant of all its citizens without prejudice. The current government of Canada has divided its citizenry into those who approve abortion and those who do not, while punishing the latter for their legitimate moral convictions.

There are a number of serious problems here. First of all, a Canadian woman does not have a "right" to abortion, not even legally. In Canada, abortion is devoid of any legal regulation. Secondly, a particular political party should not impose its peculiar ideology on all Canadian citizens. Thirdly, such action blatantly contradicts Canada's *Charter of Rights*. Finally, being pro-life should not be regarded as something so wrongheaded that government grants to students who are pro-life should be withheld from them. Pro-life students are being victimized not because they are doing something wrong, but actually because they are doing something right, namely, supporting the lives of all their fellow citizens.

Although the government's position in this matter amounts to something far worse than racism, there is little protest against it. Being in favor of abortion has become the unofficial law of the land, in violation of the laws supporting life that had been previously established by democratic processes.

There is another side of this problem, apart from students who are unfairly treated. It has to do with the governmental officials who enforce this clear example of discrimination. Where is their integrity? Without their realizing it, they are contributing, though perhaps unwittingly, to the moral erosion of society. Unlike Saint Thomas More who refused to attest to immorality, today's bureaucrats seem to be mindlessly carrying out whatever they are asked to do. In the 1962 Author's Preface to *The Screwtape Letters*, C. S. Lewis offers his own vision of Hell where today's greatest evil takes place. It does not transpire in concentration camps, he avers,

> **but is conceived and ordered (moved, seconded, carried, and minuted) in clean, carpeted, warmed,**

> *and well-lighted offices, by quiet men with white collars and cut fingernails and smooth-shaven cheeks who do not need to raise their voice. Hence, naturally enough, my symbol for Hell is something like the bureaucracy of a police state or the offices of a thoroughly nasty business concern.*

A pro-life student who is denied funding for a summer job by the government precisely because of his pro-life views is far better off than the bureaucrat who carries out the discriminatory orders of his superiors. The good name of men and women, as Shakespeare has stated, *"Is the immediate jewel of their souls".*

> *He who steals my purse steals trash . . . But he that filches from me my good name robs me of that which not enriches him and makes me poor indeed"* (Othello, Act 3, scene 3, 155-161).

Socrates, the Father of Moral Philosophy held that it is better to suffer an injustice than to commit one (*Gorgias*). Pro-life people will continue to suffer injustices, even those that are worse than racism, but it can strengthen their character and help them to see even more clearly which side is on the side of the Angels.

*Father, forgive them, for they know not what they do.*

# Vengeance is not Justice

Rioters are savvy enough to call for justice, not vengeance. They know that justice is a great value, whereas vengeance is essentially barbaric. They understand only too well that they would gain no support whatsoever if they were clamoring for vengeance. Unfortunately, their rhetoric does not represent what they are really calling for. They recognize that justice is a worthy ideal, but are in no mood to work for it. Placards reading "Abolish the police," "Defund the police," "One bad cop, all bad cops," for example, do not serve the cause of justice. Vengeance is easy and immediate; justice is difficult and requires time.

The difference between justice and vengeance relates to the difference between anarchy and civilization. History shows us that the road from "frontier justice" or "vigilante justice" is long and hard. It requires an extended period of education and the cultivation of virtues such as temperance, diligence, patience, fair-mindedness, and moral courage. In a word, the establishment of the halls of justice requires an institution. Vengeance requires nothing more than the thoughtless release of anger.

Vengeance is a species of anger, the second of the Seven Deadly Sins. It represents a form retaliation that is excessive and therefore contrary to justice which requires a careful balance between a perceived wrong and its appropriate redress. Justice is one of the cardinal virtues. Plato referred to it as the health of the soul. For Augustine, justice means giving everyman his due. For Aquinas, it is a sustained or constant willingness to extend to each person what he or she deserves (ST, IIa,IIae, 58.1). For Abraham Lincoln, *"**Slavery is founded in the selfishness of man's nature – opposition to it is love of justice.**"*

The essential problem with anger is that it operates out of control. Justice tempers anger so that it is able to operate with control. Control is needed to ensure that justice can function as a virtue. Rev. Martin Luther King, Jr. spoke well when he stated that

> *Man must evolve for all conflict a method which rejects revenge, aggression and retaliation. The foundation of such a method is love.*

George Washington warned that revenge, a form of vengeance, can easily make matters significantly worse:

> *The alternate domination of one faction over another, sharpened by the spirit of revenge natural to party dissension, which in different ages and countries has perpetrated the most horrid enormities, is itself a frightful despotism. But this leads at length to a more formal and permanent despotism.*

History is rife with horrific examples of vengeance. During the World War II, Erich Priebke was a German mid-level SS commander in the SS police force of Nazi Germany. On March 24, 1944, he commanded the unit that killed 335 Italian civilians in retaliation for a partisan attack that killed 33 German soldiers. At that time, Germany had a "ten to one" policy, meaning that ten Italian civilians should be killed for every German killed. In a very strange twist of justice, although Priebke was convicted of war crimes in 1996 for the massacre, the trial focused on the 5 deaths that went beyond

the 330 in accordance with the "ten to one" rule. Therefore, his actions could not be justified on the basis of "obedience to official orders". In the German mind, 330 deaths might be justified, but 5 more was over-kill. Vengeance, however, is over-kill from the beginning. After the defeat of Nazi Germany, Priebke fled to Argentina where he lived for nearly 50 years before he died in 2013 at the age of 100.

Christians are advised to seek justice and avoid vengeance, ***Never take your own revenge, beloved, but leave room for the wrath of God, for it is written, 'Vengeance is mine, I will repay*** (Romans, 12:19).

It is written in Deuteronomy 32:35:

***Vengeance is Mine, and recompense; their foot shall slip in due time; for the day of their calamity is at hand, and the things to come hasten upon them.***

We can extract from these words that God will vindicate the righteous and punish the wicked. He, and He alone, judges with perfect justice and perfect mercy. At the same time, we are asked to forgive, not avenge, an action that is obscured by vengeful emotions.

It is easy to give in to anger. But anger blocks justice. Vengeance is a spontaneous outburst. It seeks immediate satisfaction. In the face of a grievous wrong, the desire for vengeance rises quickly to the surface. This is something that we can all understand. But justice is needed so that things do not degenerate into savagery, as in the case of the 335 Italian civilians who were murdered. Justice demands that we rise about the emotion of the moment and put all the relevant factors into perspective. Justice is the civilized way of doing things because it is comprehensive. Moreover, justice bears upon the future. It establishes a precedent for others to study. It welcomes fair-minded people who dedicate their lives to its continuation. Vengeance is personal; justice is supra-personal. Vengeance is for now; justice is for tomorrow and tomorrow and tomorrow.

There will continue to be instances of injustice even at the hands of those who have sworn to uphold it. Being prone to error, however, is common to all professions. But the proper response is to reform the institution, not dismantle it. Reform brings about hope; dismantling leads to chaos. And chaos cannot be the ground from which a new and better civilization can arise.

Much more education in morality is needed to convince people at large that institutionalized justice exists for the benefit of everyone. Vengeance benefits no one.

# The Submergence of Philosophy

In genius and influence, Abu Hamed Mohammad Ghazali (1058-1111), according to Christopher Dawson, most resembles that of St. Thomas Aquinas. This is, indeed, high praise. This Persian scholar's most famous work, however, is *The Destruction of Philosophy* (*Tehâfat el Falâsifah*). As a Moslem thinker, he saw clearly the fundamental incompatibility between the Moslem faith and the Greek conception of the universe as an intelligible order that can be penetrated  by human reason. He would not succeed, nonetheless, in destroying philosophy. But he did succeed, to a certain extent, of submerging it.

In our own day, philosophy remains submerged because it is incompatible with the reigning ideology of political correctness. The absence of philosophy in the public forum prevents a view of reality that everyone can share. Ideologies are limited to a partisan group. Without a universal truth, particular groups will remain at odds with each other. Philosophy is the search for, and to a certain extent, the discovery, of truth. Without a unifying philosophy, people remain divided, one tribe setting itself against another tribe.

Logic is an essential part of philosophy. It abhors contradiction and demands consistency. Racism, therefore, is racism no matter what race it unjustly demeans and degrades. If all rectangles are four-sided, then every particular rectangle must be four-sided, including those that are square, rhomboid, or trapezoid. It is inconsistent for any race to assume a racist attitude toward another race simply because that race is different or has either exercised or suffered the injustice of racism.

Nobel laureate Albert Camus once stated that we must find a way in which we are neither executioners nor victims. His proposal for an even playing field is perfectly consistent with an over-arching philosophy of humanity: all men are created equal, and no race is superior to another.

A crucial question concerning the turmoil that abounds in today's world is whether "Black Lives Matter" is a realistic and effective tool in combating the evil of racism. Philosophy must be called upon to deal with this important question. The fact that it is submerged poses a problem, for it is only the breadth of philosophy that can expose the narrowness of an ideology.

Cardinal Wilfred Fox Napier, himself a black man, and archbishop of Durban South Africa, has stated that

> *a brief study of the founding statement of "Black Lives Matter"' indicates the movement is being hijacked by the interests and parties committed to dismantling the very values, structure and insti-*

*tutions which have over the centuries undergird the best civilizations and cultures!*

The Cardinal, together with a rising number of other people of color, have denounced BLM for its renunciation of

the nuclear family, its embrace of the LGBTQ+ consortium and its promotion of abortion. They represent tangible proof that Black Lives Matter is divisive even among blacks. Rev. Napier questioned whether black lives matter even to the organizers of Black Lives Matter. He cited their indefensible allegiance with Planned Parenthood.

> ***Is there any good reason,*** Cardinal Napier remarked, *other than political correctness, why abortion is not defined as & declared immortal & illegal, as THE hate crime of our era?*

Absolute silence concerning the protection of black babies in the womb does not, logically, show that black lives matter.

In the United States, there are 138 abortions for every

1,000 live births. But among blacks, the figure is 501 abortions for every 1,000 live births. Logic indicates that if black lives mattered, BLM would show some concern for the disproportionate rate of abortions among people who are black. New York Health City health statistics, for example, show that more black babies are aborted than are born each year. Yet, Alicia Garza, a co-founder of BLM states that *"reproductive justice [meaning abortion] is very much situated within the Black Lives Matter movement."*

Bishop Joseph Strickland, of Tyler Texas, has condemned BLM because of its announced threat to the good of society.

On Independence Day (2020), he cited a BLM statement declaring its plan to *"disrupt the Western-prescribed nuclear family structure requirement"*. Bishop Strickland states that the BLM organization

> *"fails to acknowledge that the breakdown of the nuclear family, which disproportionately affected blacks in America, was at the heart of the downward spiral of crime, poverty, and dependence in which many blacks found themselves."*

 Ryan Bomberger, a man of color, has inaugurated Radiance Foundation, a life-affirming foundation. He posted on his website, "Top Ten reasons I'll never support the #Black Lives movement".

A co-founder of Black Lives Matter Toronto, a Black Muslim named Yusra Khogali, has argued, as we have mentioned before, that white people are "recessive defects" and mused about how their race could be "wiped out". She has called Prime Minister Justin Trudeau "a white supremacist terrorist and has urged crowds to "rise up and fight back".

The discrepancy between logic and ideological rhetoric has given a great deal of space for its reasonableness, including violence to both people, property, and to language itself. One can understand the anger of some people and how their anger gives rise to a less than temperate reaction. That belongs to the field of psychology. These people need help, not governmental control. It is more difficult to understand how people who should know better and have not been angered by injustice, can defend the BLM position on a philosophical basis.

Although submerged, philosophy is not dead and retains is reasonableness. But it does need to be resuscitated before it can benefit people and provide a basis for universal brotherhood. Anger must subside and dialogue must begin. That is a tall order, but it is a necessary one. We need people of courage, such as Cardinal Napier, Bishop Strickland, and Ryan Bomberger, to lead the way. They are truly valiant, for they are willing to surrender repose in order to disseminate truth.

# Are We Still One Nation Under God?

After visiting America, G. K. Chesterton asked himself the question, *"What makes America peculiar?"* He answered his own question with accustomed perspicacity:

> *America is the only nation in the world that is founded on a creed. That creed is set forth in the Declaration of Independence . . . It enunciates that all men are equal in their claim to justice, and that governments exist to give them that justice, and that their authority is for that reason just.*

According to Mortimer Adler, in his book, *We Hold These Truths*, the Declaration is, *"in the most profound sense, a preface to the Constitution, more fundamental politically than the Constitution's own preamble".*

That creed is set forth with sparkling clarity in the second sentence of the *Declaration of Independence*:

> *We hold these truths to be self-evident, that all men are created equal, that they are endowed by their Creator with certain unalienable Rights, that among these are Life, Liberty and the pursuit of Happiness.*

These words are considered to be the most potent and consequential words in American history. They were reaffirmed by Abraham Lincoln in his Gettysburg Address, in particular, when he spoke of "this nation, under God".

America was founded on the principle that it was under the supervision of God who is both their Creator and original Author of their rights. Therefore, as it would be repeated time and again by Presidents and members of the Supreme Court, "America is a religious nation". The opening sessions of the Supreme Court begin with the invocation, "God save the United States and this honorable Court". The words "so help me God" are included in every presidential oath since 1789.

Is America still a religious nation? The word "equal," stated in the Declaration refers to the equality of human beings as human beings as well as their equal entitlement to justice. But it does not refer to equality of philosophy or equality of opinion. Unfortunately American liberalism has extended the notion of equality to religion and non-religion. This is an **error of considerable magnitude**, for it displaces America as a religious nation, exchanging it for one that is either equally agnostic (not knowing whether or not God exists) or atheistic (denying God's existence).

In *Torcaso v. Watkins* (1961), the Supreme Court specifically listed "Secular Humanism" as a religious viewpoint. Justice Hugo L. Black, writing for the majority, stated that ***"Neither a state nor the Federal Court . . . can aid those religions based on a belief in the existence of God as against those religions founded on different beliefs."*** In footnote 11, Black clarified what he meant by religions based on "different beliefs." He identified "Secular Humanism," which does not believe in God, as a religion. This was not the only time that the Supreme Court elevated a nonreligion to the status of a religion. A Seventh Circuit Court, in *Kaufmann v. McCaughtry* (2005), affirmed that the Supreme Court has recognized atheism as equivalent to a 'religion' for purposes of the First Amendment on numerous occasions.

According to *McGowan v. Maryland* (1961), religion is equated with ***"an aspect of human thought and action which profoundly relates the life of man to the world in which he lives"***. In 2005, the Court reiterated the notion that religion should not be defined narrowly (*McCreary County, Ky, v. ACLU, 545 U.S.*). In dissent, however, Justice Antonin Scalia made the comment that it is ***"demonstrably false"*** that *"the government cannot favor religion over irreligion"*. He could have echoed the words of John Adams, America's second president, who, in 1789 said,

> ***Our constitution was designed only for a moral and religious people. It is wholly inadequate for the government of any other.***

In *United States v. Seeger* (1965), the Supreme Court held that non-theistic viewpoints can qualify as religious as long as they "occupy the same place in [a person's] life as the belief in a traditional deity holds". In a similar ruling (*Welsh v. United States,* 1970), the Court stated that a non-theistic viewpoint can be regarded as religious if it occupies ***"a place parallel to that filled by God in traditional religious persons."*** Nonetheless, it may be argued, belief in God and non-belief in God are disjunctive categories. They are radically different nor are they parallel to each other with respect to what is traditionally understood by religion and worship, no matter how comfortable a person may be with his own non-theistic position.

**Theism and atheism are not equal**, neither politically nor philosophically. Theism refers to a being that is believed to be real, a view supported by Aristotle through a long list of eminent thinkers and, in general, by the majority of people in all cultures throughout history. Atheism, as the word indicates, is a negation, the absence of any belief in God, the view that God is not real. There can be no proof, however, for the non-existence of God. Atheism is a privation. Therefore, it cannot be considered equal to something that is not a privation. Blindness is not equal to sightedness even though they both pertain to the eye. *"Light and darkness have nothing in common,"* to quote St. Paul.

An insidious problem arises when a privation is identified with its correlative perfection. The two do not reside peacefully side-by-side. The privation attempts to overcome the perfection. For example, atheists often classify theists as *"closed minded"* or *"superstitious"*. Sigmund Freud held that religion is a neurosis. Karl Marx contended that religion is *"the opium of the people"*. Members of the LGBTQ group routinely vilify heterosexuals as *"homophobic"*. Pro-abortionists castigate those who defend life in most derogatory terms. The sexually promiscuous often deride chaste people as *"uptight," "Victorian," "prudish,"* or worse. Some theater owners have received death threats for scheduling the movie, *Unplanned*. Journalist Charles Krauthammer referred to this phenomenon as *"defining deficiency up"*. It is more like granting deviancy undue power.

A startling example of equating privation with perfection occurred in 1998 at Gallaudet University, a school for deaf and hard of hearing individuals, when students barricaded the campus gates and insisted on being given a deaf president. Elisabeth Zinser, who was not deaf, had been installed as president. Due to extreme pressure from students, faculty, and alumni, she resigned from her position within a week of her appointment and was replaced by a president who was deaf. Some of the married students, solidly committed to a "deaf community," stated that if they had a child who could hear, they would deafen it.

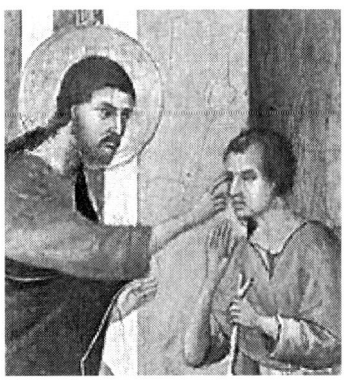

When non-equals are forced into equality with equals, an unstable situation ensues in which the natural order of things is inverted. The American Civil Liberties Union (ACLU) has sued to have the words "under God" removed from the pledge of allegiance. This is an attempt to supplant America's founding creed. But a godless world is not better than a world where a belief in God is both practiced and protected. John L. McDermott, J. D. has provided a careful analysis of Supreme Court decisions justifying the title of his book, *How American Law Lost God* (2012).

> ***In less than 150 years,*** *he writes,* ***America has taken an erroneous journey from a system of laws based on Christian principles and the natural law to morally vacuous law based upon legal positivism/relativism.***

The searing divisions on every level of morality that transpire in contemporary America are clear signs that the notion of unity under God is and has been for some time under serious attack. David McCullough, a two-time winner of the Pulitzer Prize as well as the National Book Award, has remarked that *"we need history as much as we need bread or water or love"*. His point is worth pondering, if not adopting. We, as a nation, have sorely under-estimated the wisdom of our founders as we strayed from the moral and religious principles on which America was founded. We would do well to reflect on the words of William H. Marnell, author of two highly acclaimed books, *The First Amendment* and *Man-Made Morals*. In his book, *The Good Life of Western Man* (1971), he makes the following tribute to the American Founding Fathers:

> *It may be soberly questioned if any nation in history has ever had at one time the dedicated and unselfish service the incipient United States was given by Washington, Franklin, Adams, Jefferson, Madison, Jay, Hamilton, and the rest.*

If the United States is to be once again truly united, her first step is to honor her roots and re-appreciate her extraordinary beginning which, we may say, was granted by the providential care of God.

# Deconstruction and the Incarnation

The word "deconstruction," very much like the word "existentialism," has a certain cachet. It enjoys currency among those who want to be "hip to what is hip". It presumes to be a legitimate branch of philosophy, but its trendiness and superficiality are hardly consistent with philosophy as the perennial search for wisdom. It is fashionable among university intellectuals who pride themselves for being avant garde. For those outside of academe, "deconstruction" is regarded as a synonym for gobbledygook.

The deconstructionist begins by doubting the firm reality of just about everything. As a result, he comes to believe that certain verities that people have long taken for granted, such as morality, religion, nature, and art, have all been arbitrarily constructed and therefore need to be de-constructed. Very little remains once these verities have all be deconstructed or "erased," to employ a favorite word of many deconstructionists. There appears to be very little that is not susceptible to being deconstructed. One writer contends that *"the laws of physics are merely social conventions, like traffic laws."*

Deconstruction, therefore, is a process that opens up a vast area of freedom. Once reality has been deconstructed, individuals are pretty much free to be or to do whatever they please. Here, Jean-Paul Sartre's famous dictum comes into play: *"existence precedes essence"*. But the road to this wide open freedom is also the road to nihilism, though some deconstructionists attest that it is *"nihilism with a happy ending"*. Nonetheless, the notion of unbounded freedom has appeal for many people. Realistically, however, if we have nothing to stand on, we remain unable to move.

One important area of deconstruction is gender. Traditionally, gender has always been closely associated with male and female and its most authoritative pronouncement is in the Book of Genesis where God states, "Male and female he created them". But now, under the knife of deconstruction, "gender" is regarded as an arbitrary construct. As a result, gender becomes something that one chooses. University Professor, Judith Butler offers the following explanation:

> *When the constructed status of gender is theorized as radically independent of sex, gender itself becomes a free-floating artifice, with the consequence that man and masculine might just as easily signify a female body as a male one, and woman and feminine a male body as easily as a female one"* (Gender Trouble: Feminism and the Subversion of Identity).

The social media offers popular images of celebrities who seem to personify what Dr. Butler is saying. Consider the protean images portrayed by the likes of Boy George, Mick Jagger, Madonna, Eddie Izzard, Marilyn Manson, Lady Gaga, and various drag queens. Once gender is deconstructed, anything goes, except, of course, holding to the notion that sex and gender are intrinsic to the human being and provide a reliable basis for the Natural Law.

Boy George

Mick Jagger

Madonna

Eddie Izzard

Marilyn Manson

Lady Gaga

Butler is one a number of feminists who have deconstructed womanhood itself. Julia Kristeva, for example, maintains that *"Strictly speaking, 'women' cannot be said to exist."* She argues that although there are no women (because that would constitute a stereotype), we should keep using the term because it represents political advantages for women. Such radical feminists are not afraid of indulging in contradictions.

Nonetheless, more logically minded feminists, insist that if there is one reality that feminists must uphold, it is the reality of the feminine. Christina Hoff Sommers, a feminist in her own right, has authored a book appropriately titled, *Who Stole Feminism?*.

Nature is a stubborn reality and will not be banished by an academic trend. As Cicero said, long ago,

> ***Custom will never conquer nature; nature will always remain unconquerable" (Numquam naturam mos vinceret; est enim semper invicta).***

For Christians, the Incarnation of Christ, the Word made Flesh, is a definitive indication of the reality of the body, as well as the reality of sex and gender. It is a small wonder, then, that deconstructionists regard the logos, personified in the Gospel according to St. John, as "the enemy". The Incarnation of Christ as definitively a man is an article of faith. But the reality of nature and gender are also validated by simple observation and common sense. One's gender is usually the first thing we notice in another person and the last thing we are likely to forget.

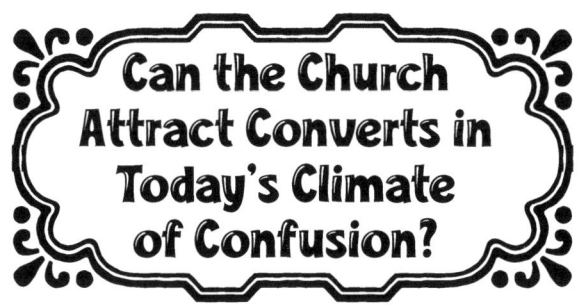
# Can the Church Attract Converts in Today's Climate of Confusion?

I have a friend who is taking the RCIA program (*Rite of Initiation of Christian Adults*). She has some legitimate concerns about joining a Church that is beset with so many problems, especially on the level of leadership. No doubt her concerns are shared by many others who are thinking seriously about becoming Catholics. To these people who are on the doorstep but are hesitating to enter the room, I would like to make four points.

1) **Historical Perspective:** The Church has been around for roughly 2,000 years and has not only survived, but has prevailed in the midst of innumerable problems. No other institution can boast of such longevity. The contemporary scene is just another obstacle that the Church will surmount, as it has done time and again throughout history. G. K. Chesterton said it best in his Orthodoxy when he penned the following words:

> *It is always simple to fall; there are an infinity of angles at which one falls, only one at which one stands. To have fallen into any one of the fads from Gnosticism to Christian Science would indeed have been obvious and tame. But to have avoided them all has been one whirling adventure; and in my vision the heavenly chariot flies thundering through the ages, the dull heresies*

*sprawling and prostrate, the wild truth reeling but erect.*

2) **The Example of the Saints:** The blessings of the Catholic Church are embodied in those individuals She has canonized as saints. They are the unparalleled witnesses of God's goodness. We do not look to the sinners to judge the efficacy of the Church, but to those who drew from it with both faith and fervor. Nonetheless, it seems that the Church is often in need of rebuilding. St. Francis of Assisi is one of the Church's most beloved ambassadors. His legacy should inspire hope for many who have their doubts about the Church. During the autumn of 1205, Francesco Bernardo prayed in the small tumbled-down church of San Damiano and heard God's command to him *"to repair the church, for it has fallen into ruin"*. All Catholics are called to repair the Church.

3) **The Importance of the Sacraments:** G. K. Chesterton stated that he became a Catholic because he wanted his sins to be forgiven. The seven sacraments that the Church offers establishes a vital and intimate connection with God. Who other than God can forgive sins? The Eucharist provides nourishment for body and soul. It is a most intimate way of participating in the Life of Christ. Holy Communion, as it is also called, is a re-enactment of the Last supper when Christ shared bread and wine with His disciples. Grace is God's life which He is eager to share with His followers through the various sacraments. We need the strength the sacraments offer in order to serve God and to avoid the wiles of the world as well as the snares of the devil. One of the most important reasons for the founding of the Church is to provide a very tangible relationship with Christ.

4) **The Church Needs You:** The Catholic Church is not

a one-way street. Just as the Church can confer many spiritual benefits on its members, converts, themselves, can make important contributions. Consider the contributions of recently declared saints such as Saint Cardinal Newman, Saint Elizabeth Seton, Saint Teresa Saint Benedicta of the Cross, and Saint Kateri Tekakwitha (all converts), along with Teresa of Calcutta and Saint John Paul II. Catholic philosophy would have an immense void if it were not for the contributions of several important converts including Jacques Maritain, Gabriel Marcel, Dietrich von Hildebrand, Edmund Husserl, and Mortimer Adler. From the arts, the Church has been blessed by the contributions of Walker Percy, William Kurelek, Sigrid Undset, Muriel Spark, Rumer Goden, Edith Sitwell, Coventry Patmore, Graham Green, and Evelyn Waugh.

We may add Mother Mary Alphonsa, Marshall McLuhan, Malcolm Muggeridge, Karl Stern, Dave Brubeck, Rev. Richard Neuhaus, Avery Dulles, and Bernard Nathanson. The list is both extensive and impressive. There is certainly room for more converts and their positive contributions are more than welcomed.

The notion of "conversion" might be misleading. The reality of conversion is more akin to a "fulfillment". Over the last 20 years, Marcus Grodi of EWTN has interviewed a long list of dynamic Catholic converts. His show is appropriately called, *The Journey Home*, indicating that a conversion is not so much a change as it is a completion. Entering the Church, for many converts, according to their own admission, feels like coming home. For others, conversion is the transition from a world of illusions to reality. Evelyn Waugh had this to say about his own entrance into the Church:

*"Conversion is like stepping across the chimney piece out of a Looking Glass world, where everything is an absurd caricature, into the real world God made; and then begins the delicious process of exploring it limitlessly."*

Conversion should not be regarded as an escape from an absurd and inconsistent world where nothing holds together. It is an embrace of the reality that God has created, which includes the pilgrim self. Muriel Spark told Malcolm Muggeridge, during a television interview that "The reason I became a Roman Catholic was because it explained me". "I wasn't able to work and do any of my writing until I became a Catholic," she confessed in the same interview. She was in her mid-thirties when she converted. Twenty years later, Muggeridge became a Catholic for similar reasons, coming to the same conclusions as Spark after a lifetime of soul-searching.

There are many obstacles in the path of the potential convert not the least of which involves one's own family. Conversion, nonetheless rests on a relationship with God. And that, in the final analysis, is what counts the most.

# Saint John Paul II Turns 100

May 18, 1920 is the birthday of Karol Wojtyla, better known to the world as Pope John Paul II. That same day in 2020 marks his 100th birthday. Of course, we know that John Paul passed away on April 2, 2005 and that only the deceased are eligible for canonization. Be that as it may, his spirit is still very much alive in the minds and hearts of the millions of people who were touched by his love and his wisdom. And he will continue his apostolate, though from afar well into the new millennium.

Saint John Paul, therefore, is a centurion in more ways than one. He is, according to the title of Jonathan Kwitny's book on the life and times of John Paul II, the *Man of the Century*. His influence was far reaching, if not unparalleled, not only in the field of philosophy, theology, and ecclesiology, but in politics. *"Without this pope,"* said Mikhail Gorbachev, the last leader of the Soviet Union, *"it would be impossible to understand what happened in Europe at the end of the 1980s."* "Man of the Century" justly applies to this remarkable human being.

But John Paul is also, according to the title of Luigi Accottoli's biography of the saint, *Man of the Millennium*. Concerning the former pope's Theology of the Body, George Weigel, who authored JP's definitive biography, predicts that it is *"a kind of theological time bomb set to go off, with dramatic consequences, sometime in the third millennium of the Church."* John Paul's good friend, Stefan Wyszynski, the great Primate of Poland told him as he entered his pontificate, that

> ***If the Lord has called you, you must lead the Church into the third millennium.***

If that is the case, John Paul mused,

> ***I must lead the Church of Christ into the third millennium with prayer and through various activities, but I have also seen that that is not enough. It is also necessary to lead my suffering . . . The Pope must suffer, so that the world may see that there is a higher gospel, as it were, the gospel of suffering.***

No doubt John Paul would brush aside the high accolades that have been accorded to him. He would defer to his earthly father. In a most personally revealing interview with French journalist, André Frossard, he spoke of the lasting influence his father had on him. As John Paul recounted, the loss of his wife, a daughter, and a son,

> *"opened up immense spiritual depths in him"* and *"his grief found its outlet in prayer".*
> *The mere fact of seeing him on his knees had a decisive influence on my early years. He was so hard on himself that he had no need to be hard on his son; his example alone was sufficient to inculcate discipline and a sense of duty.*

Discipline and duty might seem ineffective weapons against people of political power. Joseph Stalin once remarked cynically, ***"The Pope? And how many divisions has the Pope?"*** John Paul needed discipline and an unwavering sense of duty in order to fulfill his mission. He would imitate Christ and teach with the frail weaponry of truth.

At the moment of Christ's arrest in the Garden of Gethsemane, Peter drew his sword. However, Christ said to Peter, "Put your sword back into its place (Matthew 26; 52); for all who take the sword will perish by the sword." Commenting on this passage, John Paul explained that "the kingdom to which he had been called had to be won with the power of love, and with the power of truth, and only in this way."

Pope John Paul II's most definitive encyclical on truth is *Veritatis Splendor*. The title implies that truth possesses a certain light that makes it visible and recognizable. In other words, truth is discoverable. Pontius Pilate famously said, ***"What is truth?"*** That was the end of any discussion on the

topic. For John Paul, that same question should be the beginning of a discussion, and one that is fruitful. In writing the encyclical, the Holy Father was clearly aware of the fact that the modern world was siding with Pilate. America, for example, had discarded the notion that ***"We hold these truths to be self-evident"*** and turned truth into *"what is true for me"*. In other words, truth is reduced to something we invent.

Truth and freedom, intimately bound together as they are, are torn asunder so that freedom, it is assumed, can exist independently of truth. *Veritatis Splendor* explains that ***"Authentic freedom is ordered to truth,"*** that without truth there can be no freedom. Anarchy results when truth is no longer present to direct freedom to reality. ***"You will know the truth*** *and the truth will make you free"* (John 8: 32) indicates that truth is not only knowable, but is an indispensable prerequisite for freedom. It is an illusion of the most pernicious kind to believe that disregarding truth can lead to a meaningful life.

It seems that standing by the banner of truth is a comical posture. John Paul was a "fool for Christ," but certainly no fool in the conventional sense. John Paul was certainly not lacking in charisma. Therefore he was honored, praised, and applauded. But was he understood? Did his words change hearts and minds?

> *We live in a postmodern world, where everything is possible and nothing is certain,"* he wrote in *Evangelium Vitae*, *"where experts can explain anything in the objective world, yet we understand our own lives less and less."*

The world may not be blessed with another "Man of the Century". And this is why Saint John Paul II must continue to be a "Man of the Millennium".

# The Media and the Mediatrix

A mediator is someone who is situated between two parties and seeks to bring them into accord. The mediator does have a particular position of his own and operates in a completely unselfish manner. A medium, in the sense of a psychic, refers to one who establishes contact with the supernatural world. All three senses refer to a middle through which two things are brought into contact with each other.

In Catholic Mariology, Mary is given the title, *"Mediatrix"* to indicate that she, as Mother of God, is the medium through which flow all God's graces. The Second Vatican Council (*Lumen Gentium*, 61-2) states that

*she [Mary] cooperated in the work of the Savior, in an altogether singular way, by obedience, faith, hope, and burning love, to restore supernatural life to souls. As a result she is our Mother in the order of grace.*

It may be said that Mary is a Mediatrix of grace in three ways: 1) as the Mother of God, through whom Christ came into the world; 2) as the Immaculate Conception who was a sinless model for all to imitate; 3) after her Assumption through her Apparitions and constant prayers interceding for all her children. Nathaniel Hawthorne had a sense of the intermediary efficacy of Mary when he wrote the following words that are worth reiterating:

> *I have always envied Catholics their faith in that sweet, sacred, Virgin Mother who stands between them and the Deity, intercepting somewhat His awful splendor, but permitting His love to stream more intelligibly to human comprehension through the medium of a woman's tenderness.*

The contrast between the Mass Media, that delivers news, and the Mediatrix who transmits grace is a special importance for our contemporary world. News can be a vehicle for ideological propaganda. In this case, the term "media" is misleading since the Mass Media is not particularly concerned with bringing reality into harmony with the consumer. On the other hand, the grace transmitted through Mary as Mediatrix, is reliable and without a taint of deception.

The American journalist, Walter Lippmann, began his 1922 classic work, *Public Opinion,* by asserting that **"the world outside and the pictures in our heads"** are not necessarily the same. He was careful to distinguish between news and truth, suggesting that the two could coincide only in a few limited areas, such as the box score. The media had the ability, according to Lippmann, of making molehills out of mountains and mountains out of molehills.

The practice of twisting or distorting the news to serve propaganda interests is commonly referred to as "spinning". Edward Louis James Bernays, an Austrian immigrant who combined the ideas of Gustave Le Bon on mob psychology with the psychoanalytic ideas of his uncle, Sigmund Freud, is regarded as "The Father of Spin". In his 1928 book, *Propaganda*, he states the following:

> *If we understand the mechanism and motives of the group mind, is it not possible to control and*

*regiment the masses according to our will without their knowing about it? The recent practice of propaganda has proved that it is possible, at least up to a certain point and within certain limits.*

Bernays was proud of his work and is given credit for helping to make the use of tobacco and alcohol more socially acceptable to  Americans in the twentieth century. The media has gone far beyond making tobacco and alcohol more acceptable. Pornography is "adult entertainment".

Abortion is merely a "choice" while the abortionist is a "health care provider". Adultery is "serial monogamy" and same sex marriage is "equal" to that of traditional marriages. Euthanasia is "death with dignity" or MAiD (Medically Assistance in Dying). Those who have reasonable objections to such activities are dismissed as "conservative," "rigid", judgmental," or worse. As economist Thomas Sowell has written,

> *If people in the media cannot decide whether they are in the business of reporting news or manufacturing propaganda, it is all the more important that the public understand that difference, and choose their news sources accordingly.*

Saint John Paul II was very much aware of this problem.

> *The question confronting the Church today,* he stated, *is not any longer whether the man in the street can grasp a religious message, but how to*

> *employ the communications media so as to let him have the full impact of the Gospel message.*

"Spinning," therefore, is a form of propaganda achieved through providing a biased interpretation of the news, an idea, or an event. Putting a "spin" on things implies a tactic that is deceptive and assuredly less than truthful. Currently, it is a tactic that no candidate for a high political office can do without. *Spinwars* by Bill Fox and *Spin Cycle* by Howard Kurtz provide ample evidence for this contention. We now have "spin rooms" and "spin doctors" that give a certain breadth as well as urgency to this dubious practice. Joe Biden has state that 150 million Americans have been killed by guns since 2007 (Fox News, Feb. 25, 2020). This contention out-spins even the most flagrant of the spin-masters. Who could possibly believe, with just a moment's reflection, that more than 58,000 fatalities per day result from gun violence? Those who are more diligent about facts report that Biden was off by 149.9 million.

The opposition between news that defrauds and grace that is food for our souls is far from a mere academic distinction. Simon & Schuster is distributing a novella entitled *The Testament of Mary* which depicts the Mother of God as fleeing from the scene of her Son's death in fear of her own life, threatening the Gospel writers with a knife, and living as a bandit, stealing in order to survive.

We must be most careful about the news we read. But we should have no such trepidation with regard to God's grace that is transmitted through Mary, the Mediatrix of grace. The present moment calls for a return to God. The Mother of God may be needed now more than ever before.

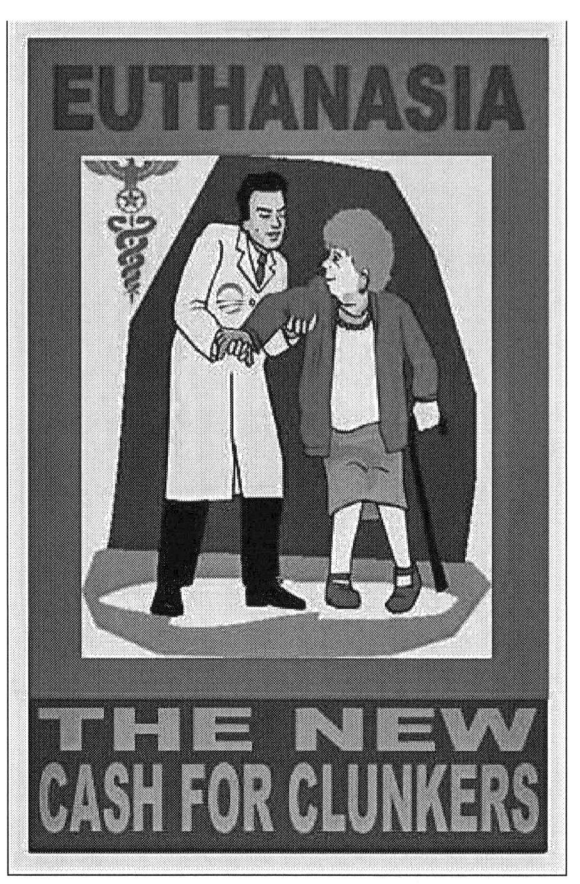
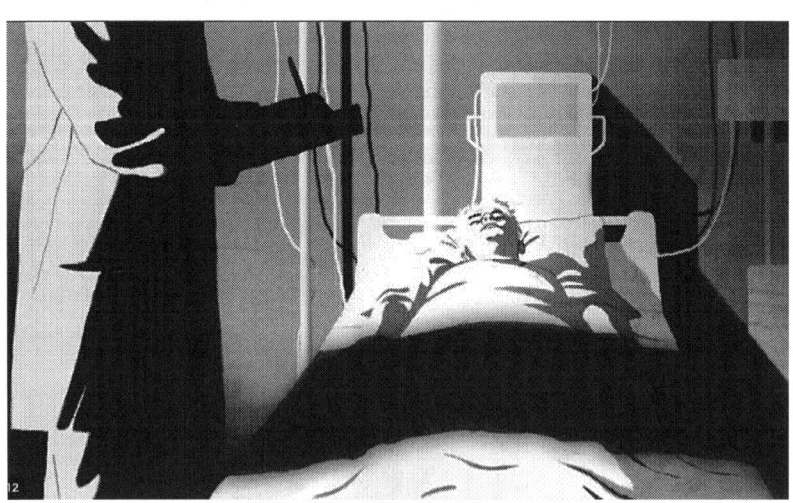

# Euthanasia and The Eucharist

The words "Euthanasia" and "Eucharist" share the common prefix (*eu*), derived from the Greek, meaning "beautiful". Their realities, however, could not be further apart. In the former case, the prefix is a deception. Induced death is not beautiful. The Eucharist, on the other hand, is a beautiful gift and is beautiful beyond words.

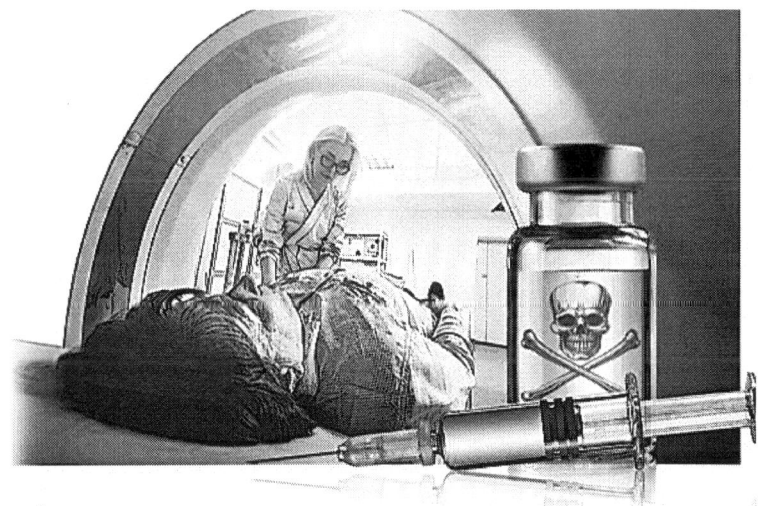

Both words represent death. Euthanasia is the deliberate death of a person. The euphemism currently employed in Canada is MAiD (Medical Assistance in Dying). The Eucharist celebrates Christ's sacrificial death in which He gained victory over death. Hence, the Eucharist is primarily about life. In fact, the Eucharist is properly described as **"The Bread of Life"**.

The Eucharist follows the transubstantiation of bread and wine. It is a consecration to a higher form of life, a life in Christ. There are three ingredients that are routinely used in MAiD: a sedative, something to slow brain activity, and something to stop the heart. There is a finality to euthanasia whereas the Eucharist inaugurates a new and fuller life.

The Eucharist provides many blessings. As Stephen Clark states in his book *Catholics and the Eucharist*,

> *The Eucharist gives us all the blessings that the death and resurrection of Christ brings to the human race* (p. 161).

The principle gift is the gift of the Holy Spirit:

> *Grant that we, who are nourished by his Body and Blood, may be filled with the Holy Spirit, and become one body, one spirit in Christ.*

Among the gifts of the Holy Spirit is fortitude that helps us to face death unafraid.

Whereas the Eucharist unifies, euthanasia separates. The promotion of the Eucharist is fairly restricted to the Catholic Church. Euthanasia is vigorously promoted in the wider secular world. As Church attendance dwindles, euthanasia is becoming more widespread. In Canada, more than a dozen people are euthanized each day, and the liberal government is proposing broader regulations (*Bill C-7*) allowing those who are suffering, but not terminally ill, to have access to MAiD. Catholics who receive the Eucharist may offer a salutary prayer for those who are failing in fortitude and hasten to open the door to death.

As an example of how the secular world is promoting euthanasia, I offer a summary of a March 7, 2020 *Toronto Star* article entitled, "Medically assisted death: Why it is good. Why it's hard." by Mirabel Palmer-Scott. In its "LIFE" section, a daughter gives an account of her 95-year-old mother who was euthanized with the approval of her children. The night before her demise, a party was given in her honor attended by her four children, three spouses, and four of her six grandchildren. The "last supper," as her daughter called it, was interrupted by the arrival of a public health nurse whose duty was to insert shunts in the woman's arms. It would be through these shunts that lethal injections would be administered.

"Mum" was diagnosed as having leukemia and was confined to a wheelchair. She did have her lucid moments and even at 95 "she remained a crackerjack with a crossword". Nonetheless, she wanted to die and requested euthanasia the very same day she was initially diagnosed. But she needed an accomplice. She asked her doctor who had cared for her for more than 10 years to assist in her passing. His eyes filled with tears when he said, "Pat, I can't do that". Nor could her caregiver oblige. "Don't do this," she protested to the daughter. "This isn't what she wants. She is too sick to know." This reluctant caregiver was said to be "highly religious". That may be the case. But her unwillingness to be an accomplice in killing also suggests that she is a good humanitarian. One does not need to be religious to object to killing a fellow human being. Religion should not be tainted as an obstacle to progress. The daughter, however, had her own misgivings: "Am I hastening my own mother to her death? Am I a horrible person? What will people think? Surely, I'll feel guilty afterwards." Two commandments were blocking the path to euthanizing her own mother: *"Honor thy father and mother"* and *"Thou shall not kill"*. These are formidable commandments and not easily swept aside. But the "sweeping" has been gaining cultural momentum.

The procedure was carried out the next day on schedule. A doctor administered the three injections and fulfilled the mother's wish. The euphemism for this act is MAiD (Medical Assistance in Dying). The word "killing" is much too harsh, realistic as it may be. Euphemisms do not alter reality, but that can help to assuage consciences.

It has been estimated that 4,235 people have availed themselves of MAiD in Canada in 2018, up from 2,704 in 2017, and 1,010 in 2016 and December of 2015. A total of 7,949 Canadians have been euthanized since its adoption on December 10, 2015. The fact that the number is skyrocketing is surely cause for concern. What will the numbers be in the coming years? If *Bill C-7* is passed, Canada will have the most permissive euthanasia regulations in the world. How far a former Catholic country has fallen from grace!

Euthanasia and the Eucharist are poles apart. They differ as light from darkness, and St. Paul has reminded us that light and darkness have nothing in common. They also differ as the desire for death and the desire for life. And yet, there may be some mysterious link between the two. Our world needs grace, fortitude and wisdom. It also need to reinvigorate its love for and appreciation for life. All these things are present in the Eucharist. The cure is available; it should be administered.

AND BEHOLD I AM WITH YOU ALL THROUGH THE DAYS THAT ARE COMING .

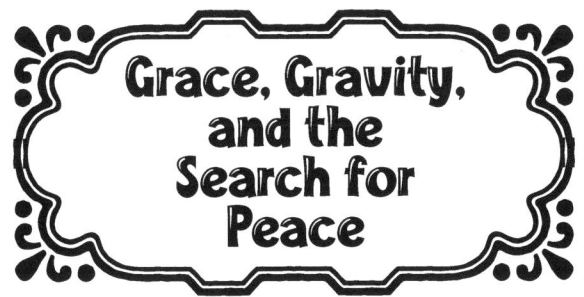

# Grace, Gravity, and the Search for Peace

Observing the protests and riots from a safe distance in my living room, the thought occurs to me that such activities are not conducive to bringing about peace. Placards stating that "there is no peace without justice" proclaim a truth, but it seems unlikely that the placard-wavers are on the road to peace. St. Augustine defined peace as *"the tranquility of order"*. A riot is the very opposite of order. If we can put our lives in order, the order that God intends, only then will we be eligible for peace. In other words, peace is far more demanding on us than we might be willing to admit. It is not obtained by shouting.

When I was in junior high school, a fellow student won an oratorical contest by expatiating on the theme, "A Bomb of Peace". If bombs can destroy, he reasoned, why can't there be a bomb that showers people with peace? His philosophy may have been indefensible, but his rhetoric was irresistible, especially at a time when fear of the bomb was a national anxiety. His audience loved the fantasy he wove that peace could be so easily provided. We are attracted to fantasy but living in reality is difficult and often disappointing.

Junior high school students, (even a champion of oratory), can be forgiven for their naïveté. The hard truth is that it is incomparably easier to destroy than to create. A child spends considerable time and effort erecting a tower of blocks, only to witness his mischievous brother knock it down with a single blow. The young builder's tears proclaim an unhappy truth about the seeming unfairness of life. Why should it be easier to be a vandal than an engineer? Life is brutally unfair. The builder, despite his efforts, ends in tears while the bully concludes his act with laughter.

Life would, indeed, be terribly unfair if we omitted one important factor from the equation — the dignity of work. We are situated between two elementary forces: gravity and grace. The former operates without any effort on our part. It weighs us down, depresses us, and is a constant source of discouragement. Grace counters gravity. It is an upward movement, a retort to the heaviness of gravity. It is the avenue, delicate as it is, to peace.

What is the meaning of life? It is to live in accordance with the line of grace while overcoming the force of gravity. Our work has great dignity because it allows us to overcome gravity with grace, the spiritual over the material, creation over destruction. If peace could arrive as conveniently as packets falling from a plane (falling with the force of gravity), we would not have earned it. Peace is something we must win. It cannot be simply given to us. And that is why, the gap between grace and gravity is a good thing, for it gives our life purpose and direction. We need this discrepancy between the ease with which things can be destroyed and the difficulty with which that can be produced, to achieve our identity and to show that we are very special creatures who inhabit this world of gravity.

Life is not a luxury hotel with little distance between desire and satisfaction. It is more like a wilderness that we are asked to cultivate into a garden. Luxury can be an enemy to life. It can be a detour that takes us off the road to peace. According to Plutarch "five great enemies to peace inhabit within us: avarice, ambition, envy, anger and pride . . . If these enemies were to be banished, we should infallibly enjoy perpetual peace".

How difficult is it to rise above the Seven Deadly Sins of which pride is its deadliest member? Saint John Henry Newman understood and expressed the answer with telling metaphorical images:

> ***Quarry the granite rock with razors,*** he wrote in *The Idea of a University,* ***or moor the vessel with a thread of silk. Then you may hope with such keen instruments as human knowledge to contend against those giants, the passion and pride of man.***

Pride is a gravitational pull away from God; humility is a disposition that welcomes a return to God. Music and poetry have wings because they soar on the magic carpet of grace.

Sin is a form of gravity; virtue follows the line of grace.

> ***No peace was ever won from fate, by subterfuge or agreement,*** wrote social reformer John Ruskin, ***no peace is ever in store for us, but that which we shall win by victory over shame or sin***

*— victory over sin that oppresses, as well as over that which corrupts.*

Returning to my observation of those who are protesting and rioting, I am not led to believe that they will achieve the great ideals — peace, justice, and freedom — that they seek. They seem unaware that these ideals are achieved only by means of victories over sin or triumphs of grace over gravity. The ideals retain their luster, but their price, seems to be out of their reach. They want peace "now," without realizing that peace require both time and effort.

On the occasion of the 17th World day of Peace (January 1, 1984), Pope John Paul II proposed, *"From a new heart, peace is born"* as his theme.

> ***Humanity's helplessness to resolve the existing tensions***, he remarked, ***reveals that the obstacles, and likewise the hopes, come from something deeper than the systems themselves.***

Neither politics, protest marches, nor progressive ideas cannot deliver peace. Peace must come from that ordered life which invites God's grace to activate the human heart, **"the innermost depth of the human person"**.

# Mary is for Everyone

The CEO of Catholic Charities of Eastern Washington, whose name we will not mention, has made the following confession to the global community.

> *I am a racist... My Catholic Church, and my Catholic Charities organization, is racist. How could they not be? Our Catholic faith tradition is built on the premise that a baby, born in a manger in the Middle East, was a white baby.*

The remark is not so much a confession, but an accusation of racism. And it is built on the baseless assumption that racism is an inevitable quality of anyone who is of a particular color, which would include everyone. This gratuitous accusation would also apply to Mary Mother of God. Our CEO is not merely confessing, but attempting to destroy, and for no reason whatsoever.

Mary has also been indicted for being white. Being white, of course, is blameless, but can we even say that Mary is "white"? Her image on the *tilma* of Juan Diego shows her to be Mexican. Is Our Lady of Guadalupe simply "white"? Other images of the Blessed Virgin show her to be Asian, African, Indian, or Chinese. Mary is for everyone. It is blasphemous to reduce her to the color of her skin.

But Mary, even as the Black Madonna, does not escape

the wrath of today's vandals. On June 22, 2020, the mayor of Breda, a city in the southern Netherlands, condemned the vandals who defaced an image of Our Lady of Czestochowa (the Black Madonna), and painted the letters BLM (Black Lives Matter) beneath it.

Paul Depla, the mayor of Breda, said that the incident was *"particularly sad for the Polish community, for which the monument is of great value"*. It is, indeed, of great value not only for the Poles but also for the Dutch. It was erected in 1954 in thanksgiving for the city's liberation from the Nazis. General Stanisław Maczek, commander of the Polish 1st Armored Division, freed the city on October

29, 1944. After the war, 40,000 inhabitants of Breda signed a petition to award Maczek honorary Dutch citizenship. When Maczek died in 1994, he was buried alongside his fallen soldiers at a cemetery in the city. The Black Madonna, a strikingly beautiful and colorful mosaic, is dedicated to the Polish soldiers of Genral Maczek who freed the city from Nazi tyranny.

It is unlikely that one can dialogue with people who know little of history, less of religion, and nothing of civility. Nonetheless incidents such as the one in Breda provide an occasion for reminding people that Mary, the Mother of our Savior, is for everyone.

The mother of Jesus was called Miriam, a common name for a Jewish woman of her time. It is a name that appears often in the writings of famed Jewish historian, Flavius Joseph. Miriam was the name of the biblical sister of Moses and Aaron. David Flusser, a Jewish author, has made the following comment concerning the name Miriam:

> *It is wonderful that the name at that time was experiencing such extensive usage. It was providential that the mother of Jesus bore the same name as many Jewish women; it is a symbol of her connection with them. It is also fortunate for the reason that, as we know, it indicated Jesus' bond with his people* (Mary: Images of the Mother of Jesus in Jewish and Christian Perspective, pp. 10-11).

Another indication of the universality of Mary comes from the pen of the Protestant novelist Nathaniel Hawthorne:

> *I have always envied the Catholics that sweet, sacred, Virgin Mother who stands between them and the Deity, intercepting somewhat his awful splendor, but permitting his love to stream on the worshipper more intelligibly through the medium of a woman's tenderness.*

The Vatican is now considering sainthood for Rose Hawthorne. She was the youngest child of Nathaniel Hawthorne.

Mary's womanly tenderness makes her more accessible to people. She is Mother to everyone. As proof of this, she has appeared to her children in Mexico, Portugal, France, Ireland, Poland, Lithuania, Italy, Rwanda, Japan, Viet Nam, Peru, Ecuador, Belgium, the United States, and the Czech Republic. This is an incomplete list, and she has appeared several times in a given country.

The Black Madonna

Mary would be merciful toward those who defaced her image. As St. Anselm has said, Mary *"was made the Mother of God more for sinners than for the just"*. This is most fitting since Christ said that he came not to save the just but to call sinners to repent. Mary leads us to God, just as she gave God to the world. She is, in the words of Raniero Cantalamessa, **"God in transparency. In her and in her life, God shines through"** (*Mary Mirror of the Church*, p. 196).

Those who strike against Mary are at the same time striking against God. Mary gave birth to God and thus was indispensable in His coming into the world. In a certain sense, rejecting Mary is a logical beginning for the rejection of God. The English poet, Coventry Patmore, remarked that Mary is **"Our only Saviour from an abstract Christ"**. Mary made it easier to know God and to worship him. She endowed him with flesh so that He could commune with others as a flesh and blood person. Flesh and blood humanity is a universal description of the human being. In this regard, she also manifests her universality.

Henry Adams, the son of America's second president said of the Blessed Virgin that *"In the bankruptcy of reason, she alone was real"* (*Mont Saint Michel and Chartres*). We are witnessing at the moment a situation that can rightly be called a *"bankruptcy of reason"*. We need Mary now, perhaps more than at any time since she gave birth to our Savior.

# Other Titles by Dr. DeMarco

*Abortion in Perspective*
*Sex and the Illusion of Freedom*
*Today's Family in Crisis*
*The Anesthetic Society*
*The Shape of Love*
*The Incarnation in a Divided World*
*In My Mother's Womb*
*Hope for a World without Hope*
*Chambers of the Heart*
*How to Survive as a Catholic in a Parochial World*
*Character in a Time of Crisis*
*The Many Faces of Virtue*
*Timely Thoughts for Timeless Catholics*
*New Perspectives in Contraception*
*The Integral Person in a Fractured World*
*Patches of God-Light*
*The Heart of Virtue*
*Virtue's Alphabet from Amiability to Zeal*
*Biotechnology and the Assault on Parenthood*
*Architects of the Culture of Death*
*Being Virtuous in a non-Virtuous World*
*The Value of Life in a Culture of Death*
*A Family Portfolio in Poetry and Prose*
*How to Flourish in a Fallen World*
*In Praise of Life*
*How to Remain Sane in a World That Is Going Mad*
*Ten Major Moral Mistakes and How They Are Destroying Society*
*Poetry That Enters the Mind and Warms the Heart*
*Footprints in the Sands of Time*
*Why I Am Pro-Life and Not Politically Correct*
*Notes from the Underground: Dialogue with a World in Disarray*
*Apostles of the Culture of Life*
*How to Navigate Through Life*
*How to Flourish in a Fallen World*
*A Moral Compass in a World of Confusion*
*Reflections on the Covid-19 Pandemic*

Manufactured by Amazon.ca
Bolton, ON